Montessori Math Workbook

A HANDS-ON APPROACH TO EARLY MATHEMATICS

PRIMARY BOOK 1

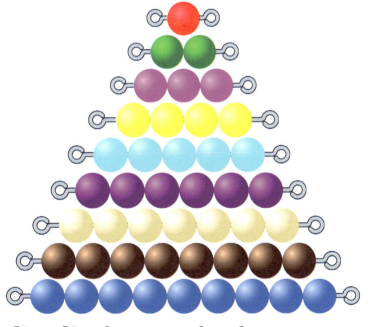

by Katie Key from raisingkingdomwarriors.com

Copyright © 2020. Katie Key. All rights reserved.

ISBN: 978-0-578-70700-6
Library of Congress Control Number: 1-8825865971

Primary Book 1

Graphics Used:
- Bead Clipart is from Bee Creative Cliparts.

montessoriforhomeschoolers.com
raisingkingdomwarriors.com

Policy Page

By purchasing and/or downloading this workbook, you are agreeing to the following terms and conditions, and I humbly request you use this workbook only under the license you purchased.

1. This Workbook is to be used only by the immediate family or single classroom of the purchaser.
2. You may not distribute by giving or selling this workbook in any format to any person outside of your immediate family or classroom.
3. You may print as many copies for your immediate family or classroom as you would like.
4. Please do not sell or re-use any or all parts of this workbook for profit.

Classroom Sets:
Please contact me at montessoriforhomeschoolers@gmail.com if you would like to place a bulk order of printed workbooks.

School-Wide Use Not Permitted:
Please contact me at montessoriforhomeschoolers@gmail.com if you would like to purchase a digital license for school-wide use or place a bulk order of printed workbooks.

Graphics Used:
- Bead Clipart is from Bee Creative Cliparts.

I trust that you will adhere to these policies, as it helps support a family like yours! I have worked very hard to create amazing resources for my family and yours, and I want to thank you for doing your part to support my small business!

With a Grateful Heart,

Katie Key

montessoriforhomeschoolers.com

Dear Parent/Teacher,

Thank you for purchasing this Montessori Math Workbook! I could not be more honored and humbled to know that you have purchased this workbook for a child. Jesus says that what we do for the "least of these," we do for Him. When you spend your time helping a child learn and make sense of the world around him or her, you are serving Jesus Himself.

I created this Math Workbook for my daughter as a solution to our need for a workbook that aligned with the work we were doing in our Montessori Homeschool environment. All of the other workbooks out there for preschool through first grade were extremely traditional, and they did not progress in the order I was presenting material from my Montessori albums. The biggest issue I found is that all of the traditional math books and workbooks for this age range moved immediately into abstract concepts, which required **a lot** of supplemental materials and manipulatives to get it to "stick" and make sense to a child not ready for abstraction.

Montessori math rightly sets a firm foundation in **concrete principles** before slowly progressing into abstraction. This workbook uniquely takes the Montessori **concrete materials** and puts them **on paper**, so your child can sit with a pencil, scissors, and glue, and concretely manipulate, touch, and visualize numbers, creating a strong math foundation using just this workbook.

This is not a "Definitive Guide to Montessori Math." This is a **workbook** that coincides with traditional Montessori math learning.

Some families or schools may choose to use this workbook as a **supplemental resource**, which was my original intention for our homeschool!

Other families may find that this workbook is a **full math curriculum**, which it can be, as I realized upon the completion of this book. I hope and pray that this workbook and the next volumes that follow will answer the need for a simple but profound way of teaching math that Dr. Maria Montessori pioneered so long ago. There are families and schools that can benefit from Montessori math concepts that may not have the funds, the space, the time, or the know-how to run a full Montessori math program with all of the materials that are necessary.

I welcome and encourage feedback! I am human, so if there are errors, please do not hesitate to let me know. If you see a way that the workbook can be improved, I welcome those comments as well. We also can *all* benefit from encouragement, so I humbly ask for you to write me your praises so I can be encouraged, and so I can share them on my sales page if you give me permission.

Enjoy this journey with your child!

In Christ,

Katie Key
raisingkingdomwarriors@gmail.com

Math Objectives Covered

Note: This workbook is an "Open and Go" Math Curriculum. Grab your pencil, scissors, and glue, and you can do any lesson in here. I do suggest using small objects as "counters" like mini erasers or beads, as well as making the number cards "tactile" by adding sand. Both of these suggestions are not vital to the success of the curriculum, but both are recommended.

In Book 1, your child will start by learning one-to-one correspondence and matching amounts to the numbers 1-10 using tactile numerals.

We will progress from there to the Montessori Number Rods, where we will introduce red and blue rods, showing that "2" can be *a single number made of two units, which is longer than one but shorter than 3.* We will introduce *larger, smaller, greater than, less than, one more/less, two more/less, addition,* and *subtraction* using the Number Rods.

After the Number Rods, we move to the Cards and Counters, where we introduce more practice with counting, one:one correspondence, and newly introduce even and odd.

Next is the bead bars, introducing a tangible material that will be around for a while to teach a wide array mathematics operations. In Book 1, we will have an introduction to addition, grouping, exchanging, and matching numerals and quantities. Children will get to "make ten" via the Snake Game.

Teen numbers are covered in depth, and we use the beads and number rods, as well as the "Teen Boards" to give a comprehensive, concrete exploration with the teen numbers.

After teens, the children explore tens visually with golden bead bars and symbolically with the "Ten Boards."

To pull it all together, children will enjoy counting 1-99 using beads and "making" each written number with the Ten Boards.

Lastly, the Hundred Board is introduced, and the children will get to see their hard work come together in a huge chart that can be manipulated many ways in this workbook.

Celebrate your child's accomplishment in completing this workbook by presenting them with the special letter found on the very last page. You will give your child specific praise for his or her hard work, and you can record the date completed for your records.

TABLE OF CONTENTS

Tactile Numerals	1
Sandpaper Number Games	43
Writing Numbers	44
Writing Numbers: Tracing Sheets	45
Spindle Boxes	48
Practicing "Zero"	53
Number Rods	54
Number Rods - Align	56
Number Rods: Second Period	61
Number Rods: Third Period	65
Number Rods: Larger or Smaller	67
Number Rods: One More or One Less	68
Number Rods: Two More or Two Less	71
Number Rods: Greater Than or Less Than	75
Number Rods and Cards	79
Number Rods and Cards: Make Ten	85
Number Rods and Cards: Subtract from Ten	95
Cards and Counters	106
Cards and Counters: Identify the Number	108
Cards and Counters: Dots and Numbers Match	109
Cards and Counters: Even or Odd	111
Cards and Counters: Even or Odd Exercise	119
Short Bead Bars: Intro	122
Short Bead Bars: Cut and Paste	127
Short Bead Bars: Coloring the Stair	128
Short Bead Bars Coloring Book	129
Number Match Game	135

TABLE OF CONTENTS

Bead Stairs for Activities	151
Give the Beads by Name	153
Beads to Number	155
Number to Beads	156
Bead Bars: Mixed Order to Mixed Order	157
Short Bead Bars Design Cards	158
Make Ten Snake Game - Intro	161
Bead Organizer	167
Make Ten Snake Game	169
Make Your Own Snake	174
Make Ten Snake Game with the Black and White	175
Make Ten Snake Game - Random	177
Child-Made Random Snake	182
Introduction to Teen Values with Beads	183
Introduction to Teen Values with Beads - Set 1	185
Practicing 11-13 with Beads	187
Introduction to Teen Values with Beads - Set 2	189
Practicing 14-16 with Beads	191
Introduction to Teen Values with Beads - Set 3	193
Practicing 17-19 with Beads	195
Beads for Teen Activities	197
Teen Numerals - Introduction Using Teen Boards	199
Teen Boards	202
Teen Numbers - Teen Bead Hanger	206
Teen Numerals - Numeral and Quantity Match	208
Sandpaper Teen Number Games	211
Writing Teen Numbers	212
Sandpaper Teen Number Cards	213
Writing Teen Numbers: Tracing Sheets	219
Teen Number Match Game	221
Teen Numbers Coloring Book	237
Teens with the Number Rods	244
Number Rods and Cards: Make Teen Numbers	247
What number is this?	252

TABLE OF CONTENTS

Introduction to Tens with the Ten Boards	255
Ten Boards	258
Tens - Numeral and Quantity Match	260
Tens: How many?	263
Finding Ten	264
Counting 1-99	265
Beads for Counting 1-99	267
Ten Boards: Counting 1-99	270
Counting 1-99 Record Keeping	273
Write the Number	274
100 Chain - Intro	279
100 Chain Exercises	281
My 100 Chain	283
100 Chain Cut and Paste	284
Hundred Board - Intro	285
Hundred Board Control Chart	289
Trace the Numbers 1-100	291
Hundred Board Fill-in-the-Blank	293
Write the Numbers 1-100	299
Book 1 Letter and Completion Certificate	301

Tactile Numerals

Directions:
Create tactile numbers using watered down liquid glue (2:1 ratio of white school glue to water), paint over the black numeral, trying to stay within the black portion. Then, add craft sand and shake off excess. Let dry.

Alternatives to craft sand: regular sand, glitter, pom-poms, felt, glitter glue.

It will be helpful to print these pages one-sided and on thick card stock paper so that you can pull them out of the workbook to use for other exercises.

*Note: If you have a set of sandpaper numbers, you do not need to make these tactile unless you choose to.

To Present:
1. Point to the star on the left hand page. Say, "This is one star. One."
2. Point to the numeral "1" on the right hand page. Trace the numeral with your pointer and middle fingers together while you say, "This says 'one.' One."
3. Invite your child to count and trace.

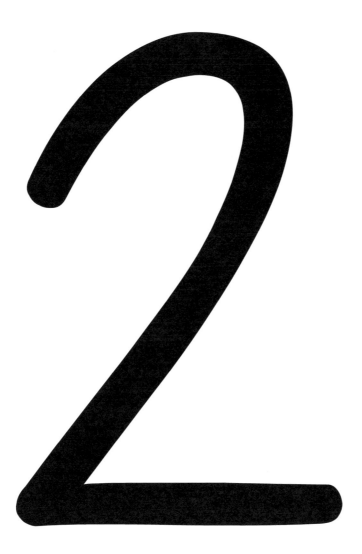

3

4

5

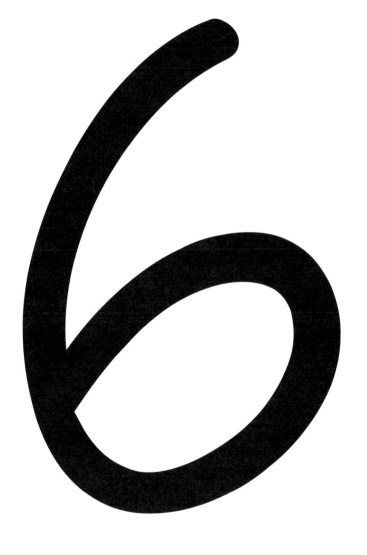

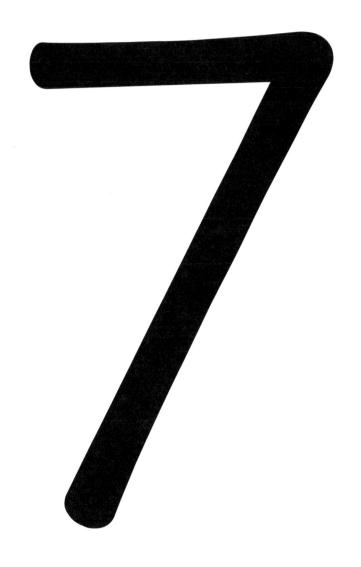

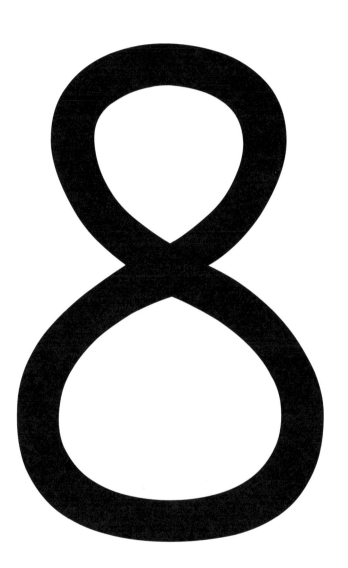

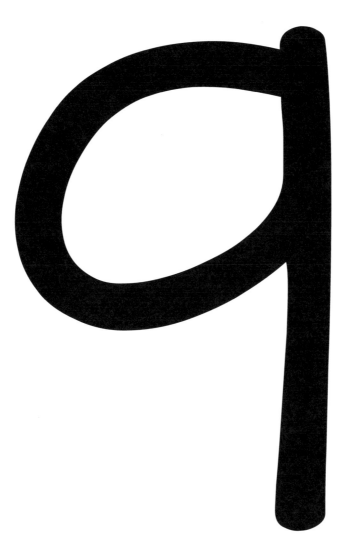

10

Sandpaper Number Games

Game #1: After the initial presentation of all of the tactile numbers, gather 10 small, identical objects to use as counters. Flip through the tactile numbers and review them in this manner:
1. Place a counter on top of the star on the left-hand "star" page. Say, "One."
2. Trace the number 1 as before with your pointer and middle fingers. Say, "This says one."
3. Invite your child to continue in this manner for 1-10.

Game #2: Remove the tactile numbers from the workbook and place them at a far location. Ask your child to fetch each number, out of order.

Game #3: Shuffle the stack of tactile numbers. Choose a random number and ask your child to identify the numeral.

Game #4: Shuffle the stack of tactile numbers. Invite your child to place them in order 1-10.

Game #5: Shuffle the stack of star pages. Invite your child to place them in order 1-10.

Game #6: Combine games 4 and 5. Shuffle both the stack of tactile numbers and the stack of star pages. Invite your child to lay out one stack in order and then match the other stack underneath each matching paper.

	Numbers	Date	Notes
Game 1	1 2 3 4 5 6 7 8 9 10		
Game 2	1 2 3 4 5 6 7 8 9 10		
Game 3	1 2 3 4 5 6 7 8 9 10		

	Numbers	Date	Notes
Game 6	1 2 3 4 5 6 7 8 9 10		
Game 5	1 2 3 4 5 6 7 8 9 10		
Game 4	1 2 3 4 5 6 7 8 9 10		

Key: Mark the numbers you have called and your child got correct with an "X." Mark the numbers you have called and your child did not get correct with a slash "/." Make sure to play again and call those numbers another time. When your child gets it "right" then make the full "X."

Writing Numbers

First introduce the "sand tray." Give your child one tactile numeral. Your child should trace the tactile numeral three times with his or her pointer and middle fingers and then draw it in sand. Invite your child to draw as many numbers as he or she shows interest in one sitting. After all numbers have been practiced many times in sand, you can introduce the tracing sheets on the next page. Record progress on this sheet with the dates you I = Introduced the activity, A = your child Attempted the activity, and M = your child mastered the activity.

	Sand - I	Sand - A	Sand - M	Paper - I
1				
2				
3				
4				
5				
6				
7				
8				
9				
10				

Writing Numbers: Tracing Sheets

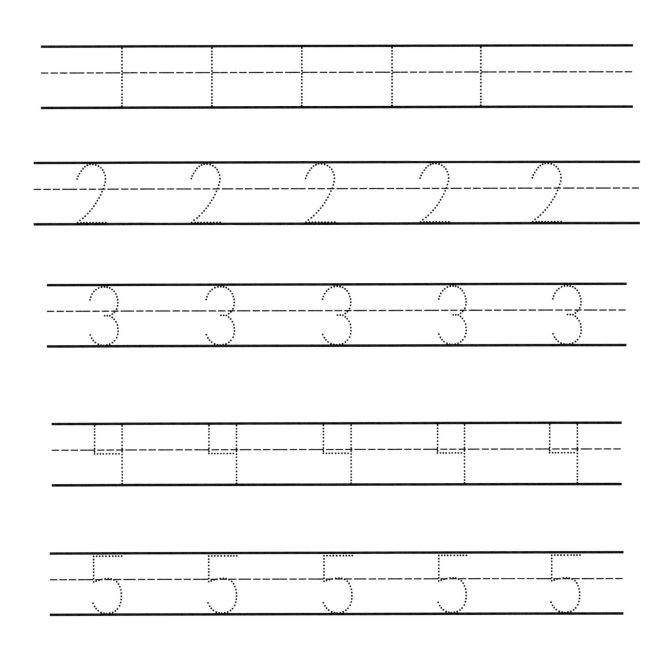

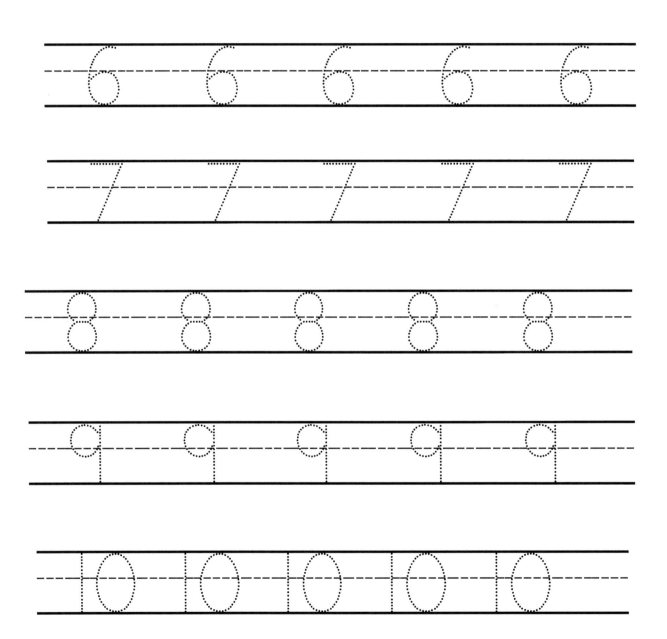

Spindle Boxes

Directions: Cut apart (or have your child cut apart) the spindles (or popsicle sticks). Practice reading and pointing to numbers 0-9 with your child first. Then, point to the numeral and read it aloud, "one." Then place one spindle and say, "one." For two and so on, point to the numeral and say, "Two." Then place two sticks one a time, counting as you do so, "One, two." If you have not done this activity in real life, make sure to practice several times before gluing the sticks into their spaces.

Introduction of "0" - At first, you should read the number zero and say, "Zero means nothing, so we will put no spindles in this compartment, and then fill 1-9 with the spindles. Then, when there is "nothing left," say to your child that "Zero means nothing. There are no spindles left to put in the zero compartment."

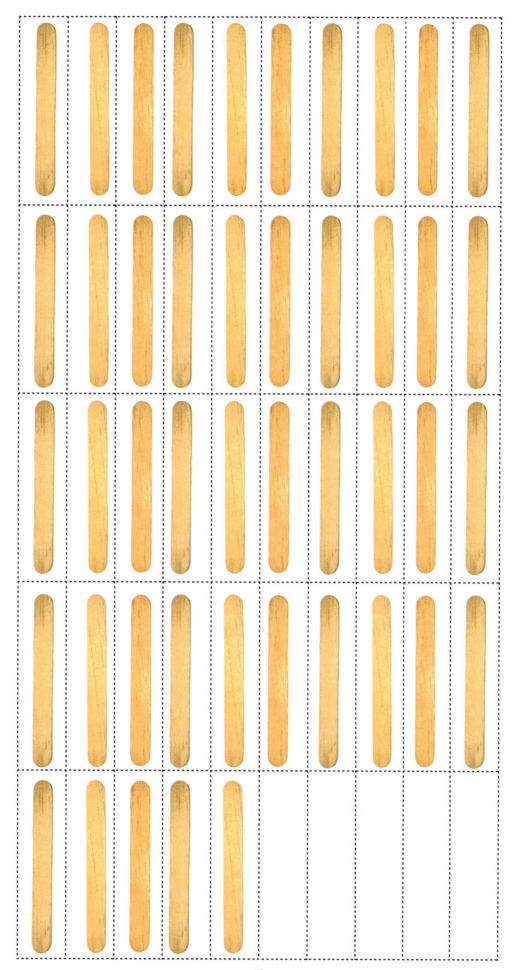

Practicing "Zero"

Directions: Play several games with your child to help him or her understand the concept of "zero."

Game #1: Jumping! Pick a number 0-10 and have your child jump that many times. When you say "zero," make sure to make a big deal out of your child not jumping. Appeal to your child's sense of humor. ("Why aren"t you jumping!? I said "zero!")

Game #2: Clapping! (Same as jumping.)

Game #3: Bring me __ toys/blocks.

	Numbers	Date	Notes
Game 1	0 1 2 3 4 5 6 7 8 9 10		
Game 2	0 1 2 3 4 5 6 7 8 9 10		
Game 3	0 1 2 3 4 5 6 7 8 9 10		

Key: Mark the numbers you have called and your child got correct with an "X." Mark the numbers you have called and your child did not get correct with a slash "/." Make sure to play again and call those numbers another time. When your child gets it "right" then make the full "X."

Number Rods

Directions:
1. Point to each rod, starting at "one." Say, "This is the rod of one." Place your finger on the red section. Count aloud, "One."
2. Point to the rod of two. Say, "This is the rod of two." Place your finger on the first red section. Count aloud as you move to each section, "One, two."
3. Point to the rod of three. Say, "This is the rod of three." Place your finger on the first red section. Count aloud as you move to each section, making sure to progress from left to right, "One, two, three."
4. Continue for all ten rods.

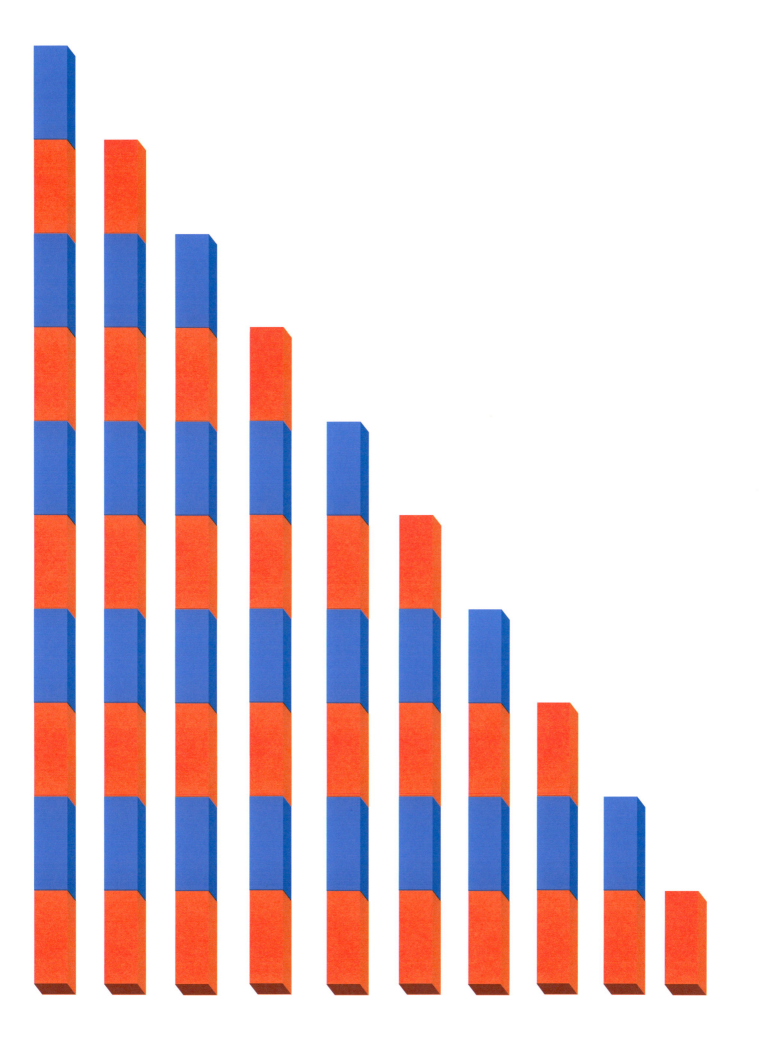

Number Rods - Align

Directions:
1. Cut apart (or have your child cut apart) the number rods 1-10.
2. Place number rods in mixed order on the table.
3. Invite your child to place the number rods in order on the next page, aligning the Rod of Ten at the top left of the paper.

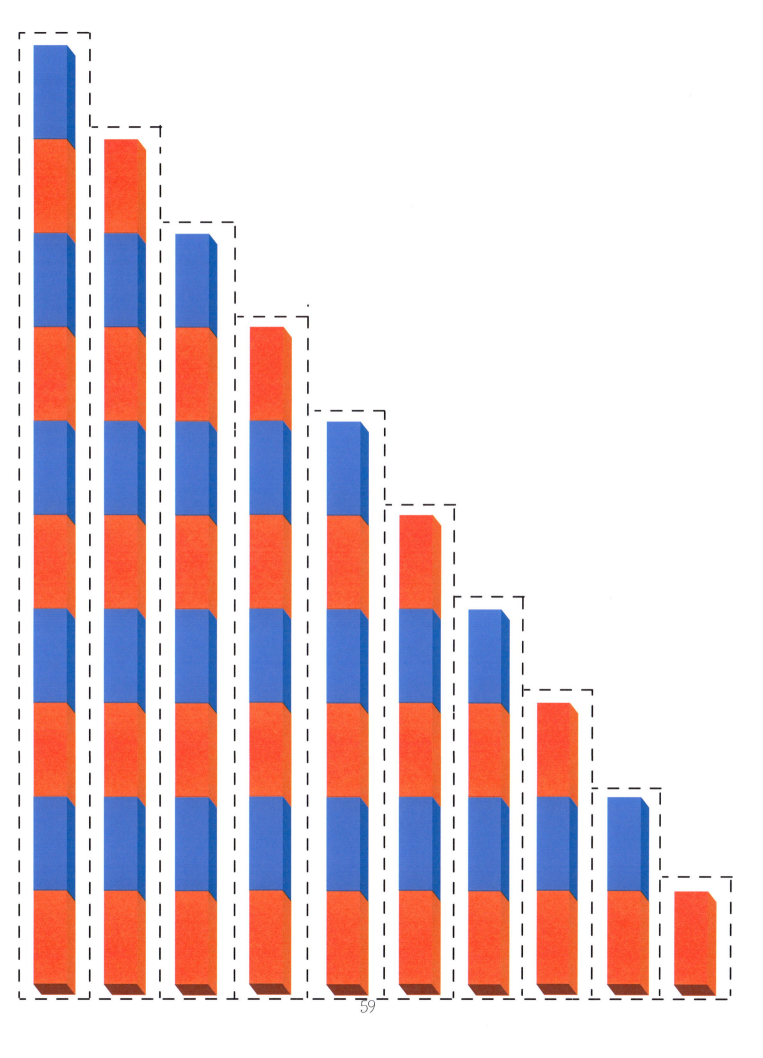

Number Rods: Second Period

Directions: Cut apart or have your child cut apart a set of number rods. Ask for each rod in turn. Have your child paste the rod into the box.

May I please have the Rod of 3?

May I please have the Rod of 7?

May I please have the Rod of 4?

May I please have the Rod of 1?

May I please have the Rod of 6?

May I please have the Rod of 9?

May I please have the Rod of 2?

May I please have the Rod of 10?

May I please have the Rod of 5?

May I please have the Rod of 8?

Number Rods for "Number Rods: One More or One Less" (p. 68) and "Number Rods: Two More or Two Less" (p.71)

Number Rods for "Number Rods: Second Period" (p.61) and "Number Rods: Larger or Smaller" (p. 67)

63

Number Rods: Third Period

Directions: Ask your child to identify each number rod. If your child is not writing yet, you can write the numbers for him or her. You can also just draw a check mark to indicate you have asked the question. This is not an activity where your child should be focused on what the written numerals look like.

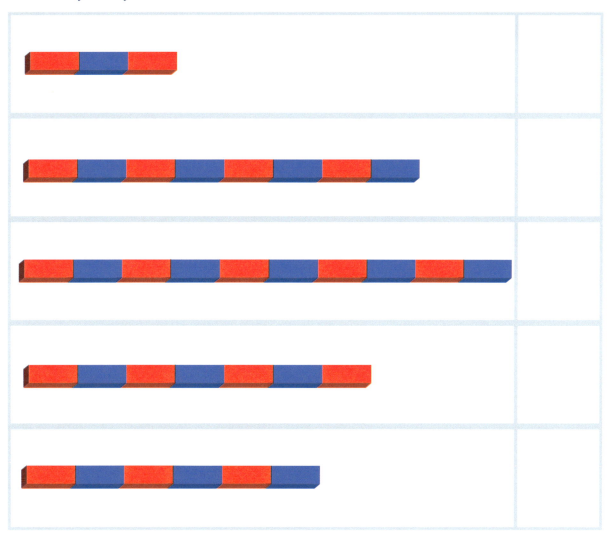

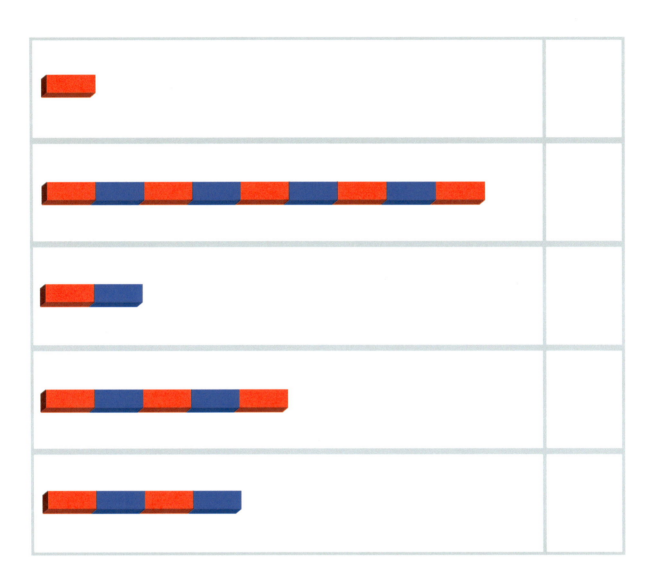

Number Rods: Larger or Smaller

Directions: Place a set of cut up number rods on the table. (Rods are on page 63.) Retrieve the Rod of 5 and place it on top of the Rod of 5 on this page, covering it completely. The Rod of 5 will be your "starting rod" for this entire exercise.
Next, mix up the remainder of the rods and ask your child for a rod that is smaller than the rod of 5. Verify that the rod is smaller by aligning it. If it is larger, invite your child to try another rod. Continue asking for a rod that is "larger" or "smaller" than the Rod of 5 until all rods are aligned.

Number Rods: One More or One Less

Directions: Place a set of cut up number rods on the table (p. 63). Ask your child for the rod that is "one more" or "one less" as indicated by the directions in the box. Do not glue these down, just have your child align the cut-out rod underneath the one printed in each box then replace to the lot on the table. Write the answer as a numeral in the box. If your child is writing, he or she can write the numeral answer. When you are finished, complete the summary sentence and read it aloud to your child.

Please place the rod in the box that is one less than this rod.

This is the rod of ___. One less than ___ is

Please place the rod in the box that is one more than this rod.

This is the rod of ___. One more than ___ is

Please place the rod in the box that is one less than this rod.

This is the rod of ___. One less than ___ is

Please place the rod in the box that is one less than this rod.

This is the rod of ___. One less than ___ is

Please place the rod in the box that is one more than this rod.

This is the rod of ___. One more than ___ is

Please place the rod in the box that is one less than this rod.

This is the rod of ___. One less than ___ is

Please place the rod in the box that is one less than this rod.

This is the rod of ___. One less than ___ is

Please place the rod in the box that is one less than this rod.

This is the rod of ___. One less than ___ is

Please place the rod in the box that is one more than this rod.

This is the rod of ___. One more than ___ is

Please place the rod in the box that is one more than this rod.

This is the rod of ___. One more than ___ is

Please place the rod in the box that is one less than this rod.

This is the rod of ___. One less than ___ is

Number Rods: Two More or Two Less

Directions: Place a set of cut up number rods on the table (p. 63.) Ask your child for the rod that is "two more" or "two less" as indicated by the directions in the box. Do not glue these down, just have your child align the cut-out rod underneath the one printed in each box then replace to the lot on the table. Write the answer as a numeral in the box. If your child is writing, he or she can write the numeral answer. When you are finished, complete the summary sentence and read it aloud to your child.

Please place the rod in the box that is two less than this rod.

This is the rod of ___. Two less than ___ is

Please place the rod in the box that is two more than this rod.

This is the rod of ___. Two more than ___ is

Please place the rod in the box that is two less than this rod.

This is the rod of ___. Two less than ___ is

Please place the rod in the box that is two less than this rod.

This is the rod of ___. Two less than ___ is

Please place the rod in the box that is two more than this rod.

This is the rod of ___. Two more than ___ is

Please place the rod in the box that is two less than this rod.

This is the rod of ___. Two less than ___ is

Please place the rod in the box that is two more than this rod.

This is the rod of ___. Two more than ___ is

Please place the rod in the box that is two less than this rod.

This is the rod of ___. Two less than ___ is

Please place the rod in the box that is two more than this rod.

This is the rod of ___. Two more than ___ is

Please place the rod in the box that is two more than this rod.

This is the rod of ___. Two more than ___ is

Please place the rod in the box that is two less than this rod.

This is the rod of ___. Two less than ___ is

Number Rods: Greater Than or Less Than

Directions: Cut apart the two sets of number rods on this page. (Tip: cut them into strips first, and your child can cut the joined rods apart.) Cut out the "less than" and "greater than" symbols. Read the statement that asks for a rod that is "greater than" or "less than," showing the large symbol card as you ask. Verify the rod your child chooses is greater than or less than the given rod by aligning it underneath the rod. Then have your child paste it on the right hand side of the box. Lastly, invite your child to copy the proper symbol by looking at the card you are holding.

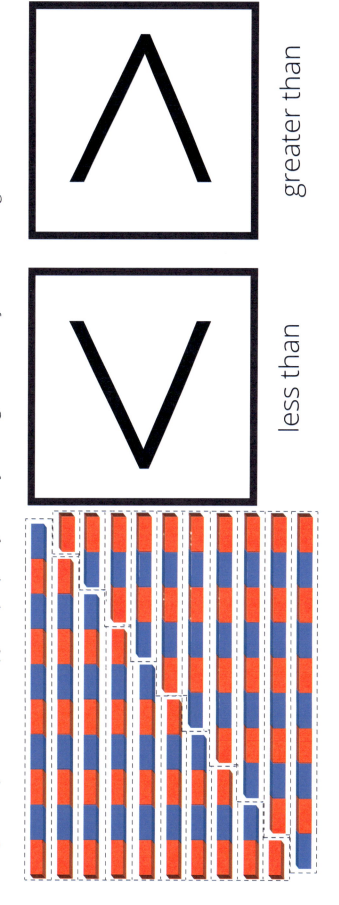

greater than

less than

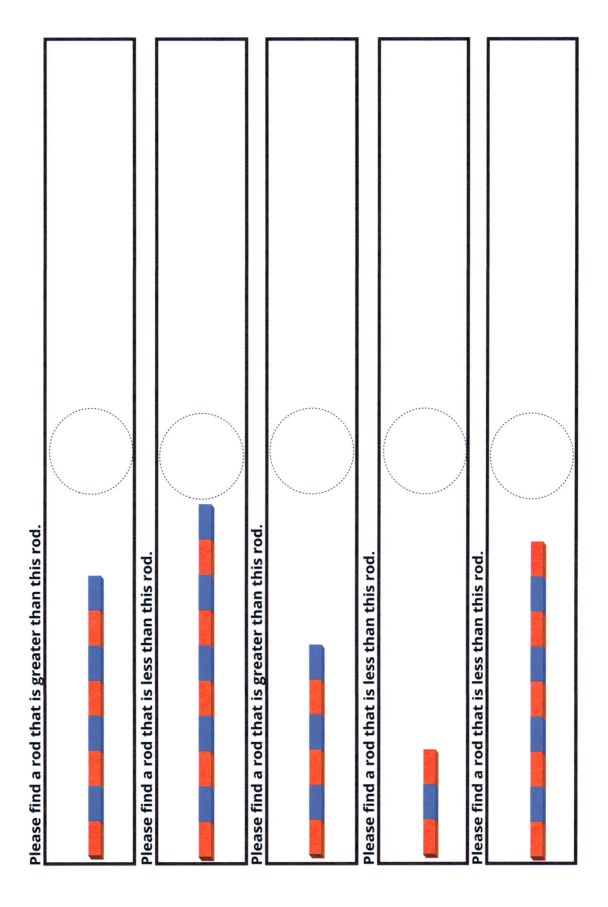

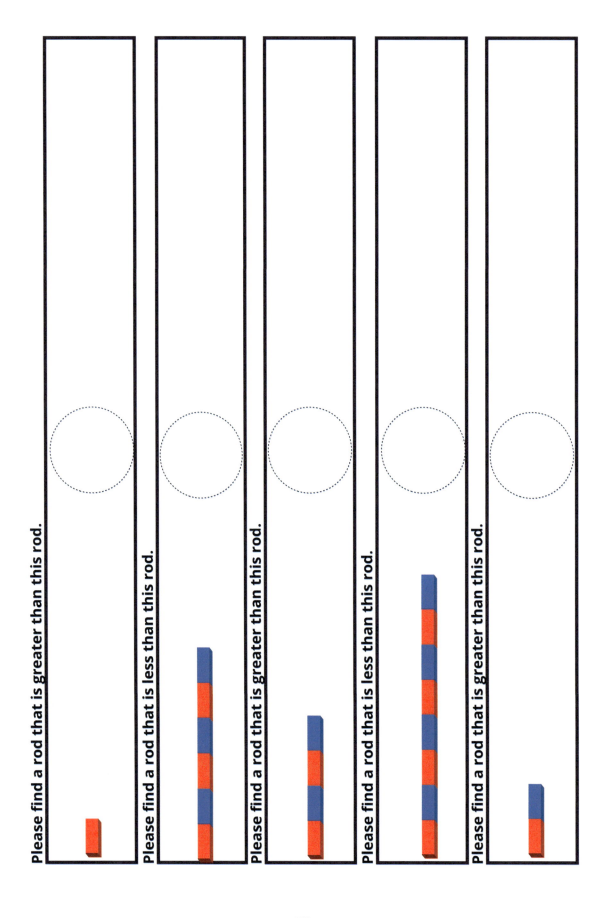

Number Rods and Cards

Directions: For the initial presentation in Problem #1, cut apart the numeral cards and place them, in order below the number rods on the next page. Pick up the number "1" and say, "This says one." Place the "one card to the right of the Rod of One in the box. Continue for all numbers, making sure to count each section of the number rods.

Directions for Practice: Problems #2-4 can be done by your child as practice problems for mastery. Invite your child to cut out the corresponding strip of number cards and place them on top of the cards below each problem, then paste them in the proper boxes.

Alternatively, your child could point to the numeral card printed below each problem and he or she (or you) could write the number in the box.

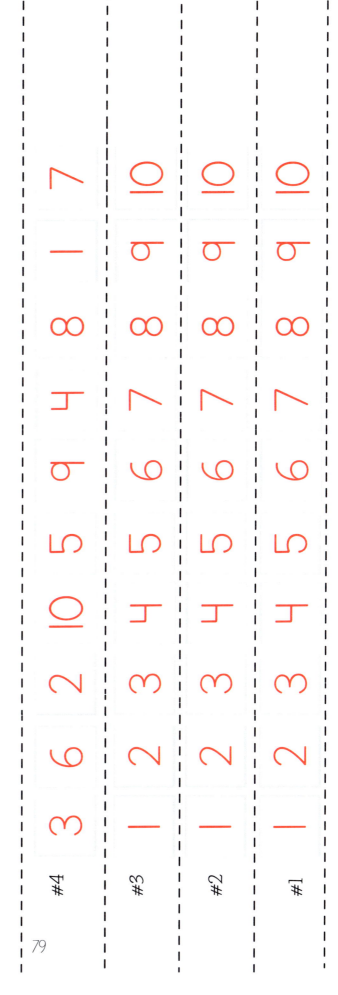

#1

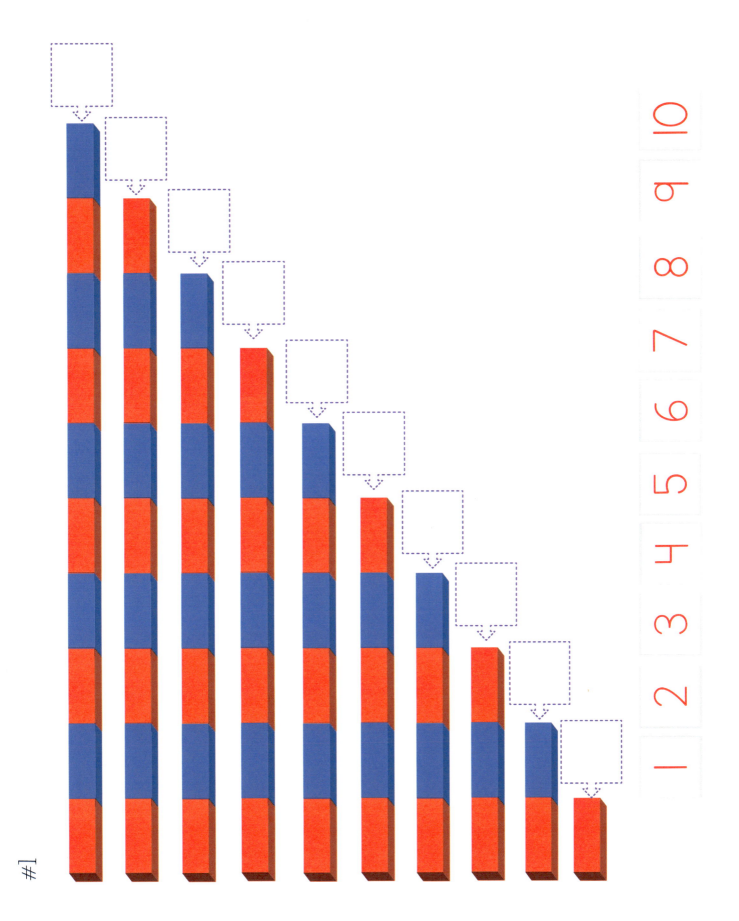

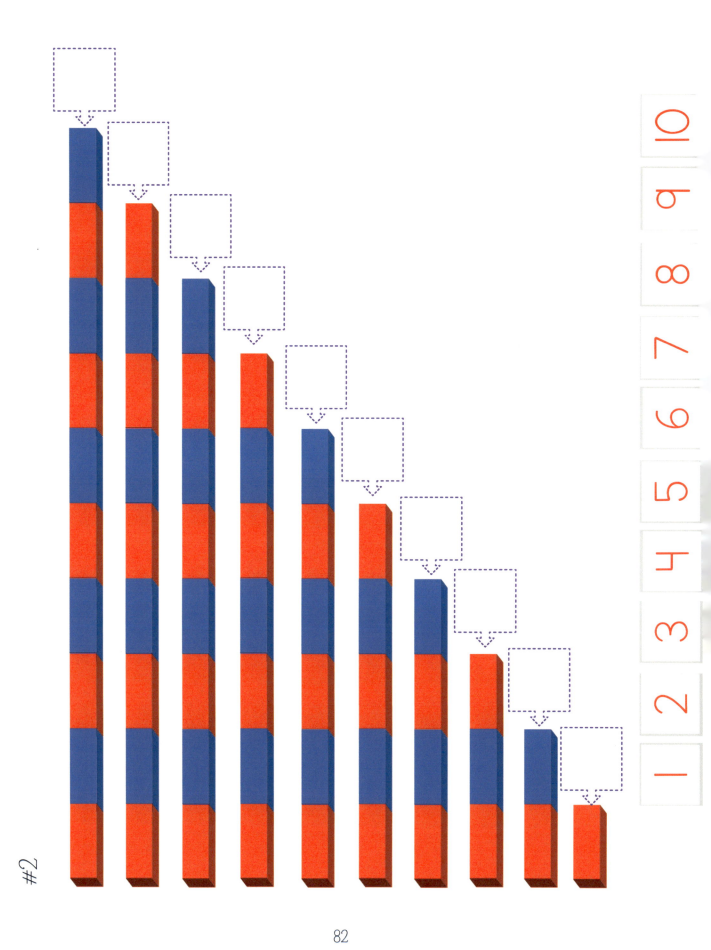

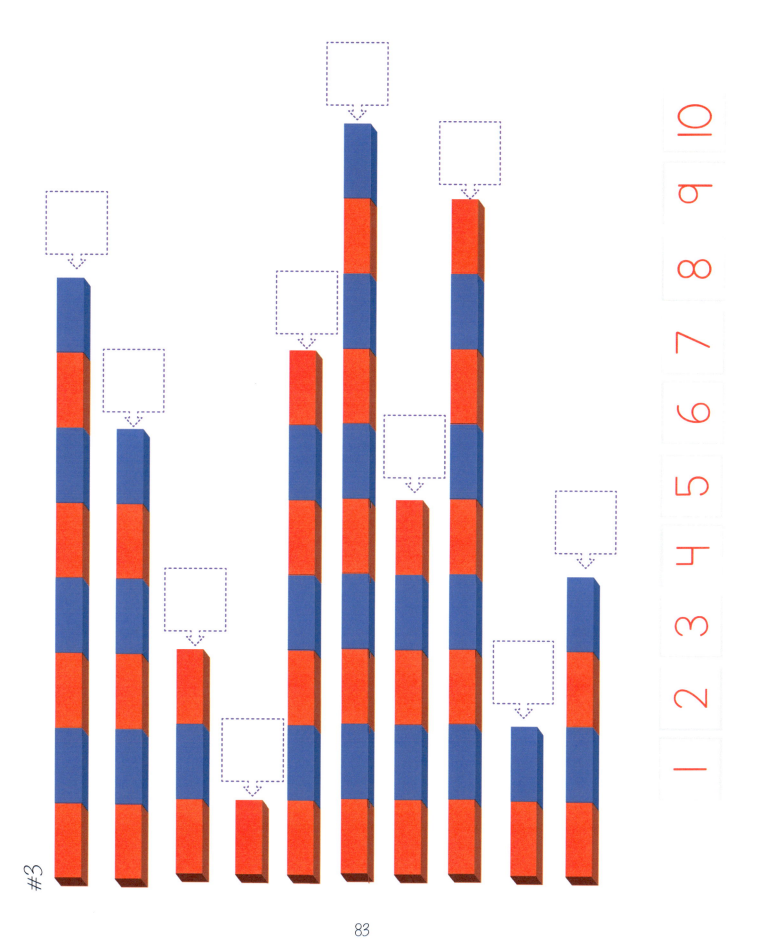

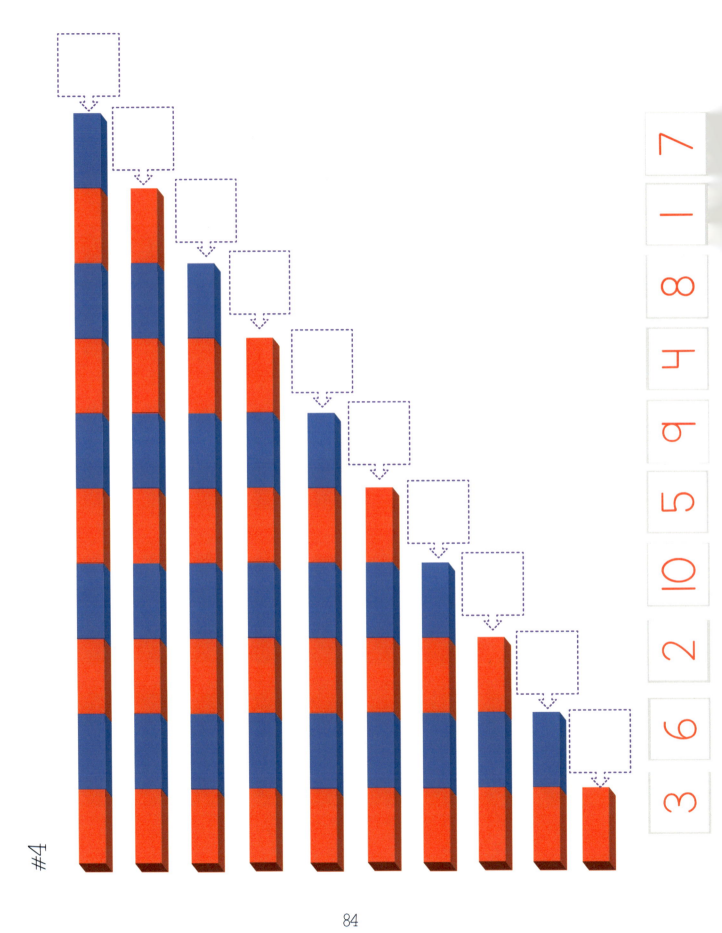

Number Rods and Cards: Make Ten

This exercise is an initial exposure to addition, without writing number sentences. Follow the dialogue of the example problem for each subsequent problem. You will need to cut apart two sets of number rods 1-9 and two sets of number cards 1-9 for this lesson.

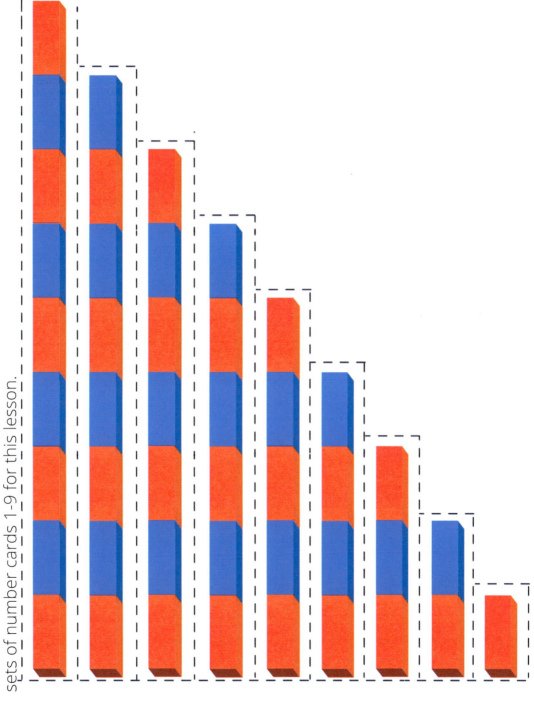

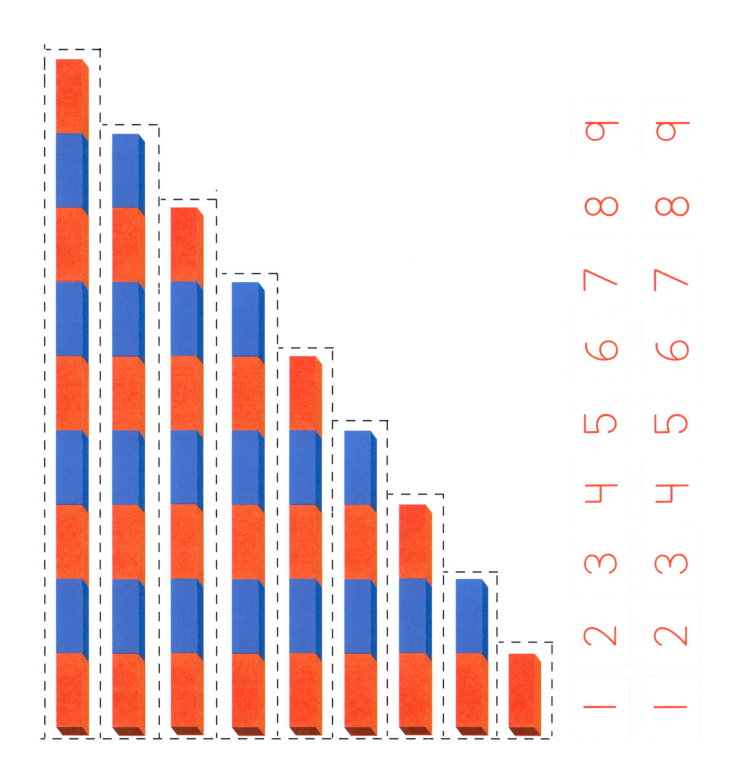

Number Rods and Cards: Make Ten

Follow this Example: Please place the Rod of 9 directly underneath the Rod of 10. [Wait.] Now place the "9" Numeral Card just underneath the last section of the Rod of 9. [Wait.] Now, place the Rod of 1 directly to the right of the Rod of 9. [Wait.] Now, place the "1" numeral card just underneath the Rod of 1. [Wait.] Run your finger along the length of the rods as you say, "Nine plus one equals ten." Lastly, run your finger along the rod of ten and say, "This is ten." Run your finger along the joined Rod of 9 and Rod of 1 and say, "This is ten." [Glue everything down when finished.]

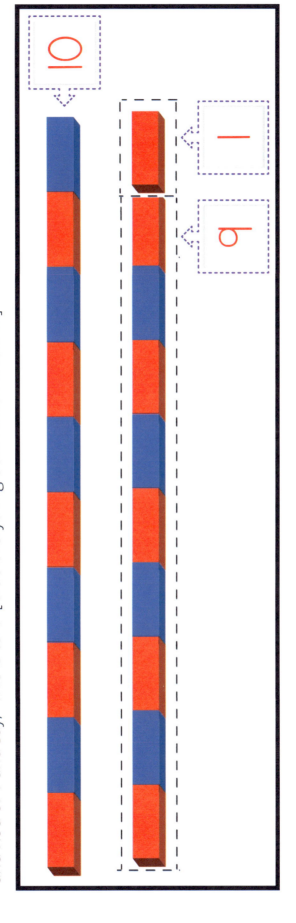

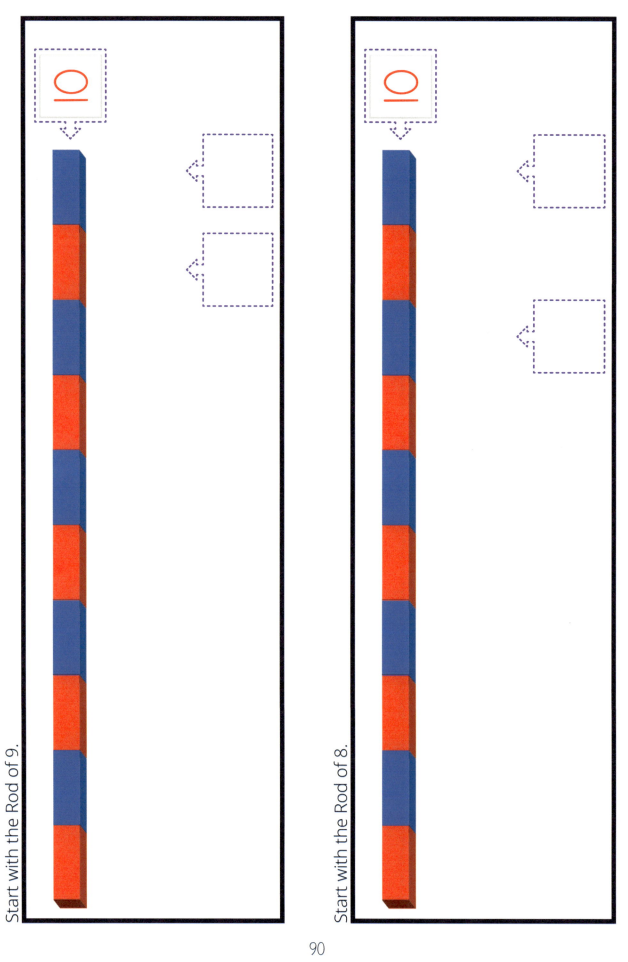

Start with the Rod of 9.

Start with the Rod of 8.

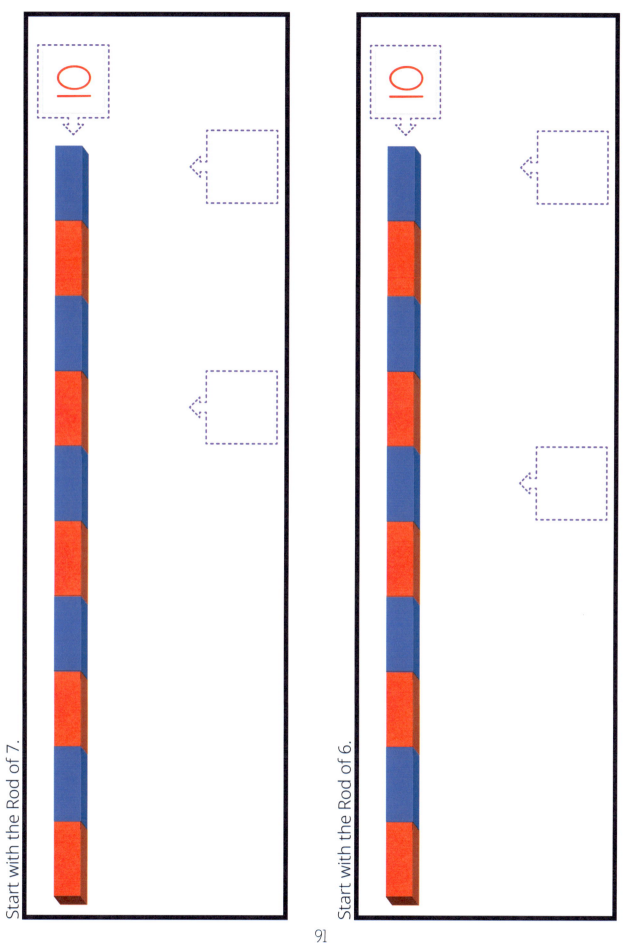

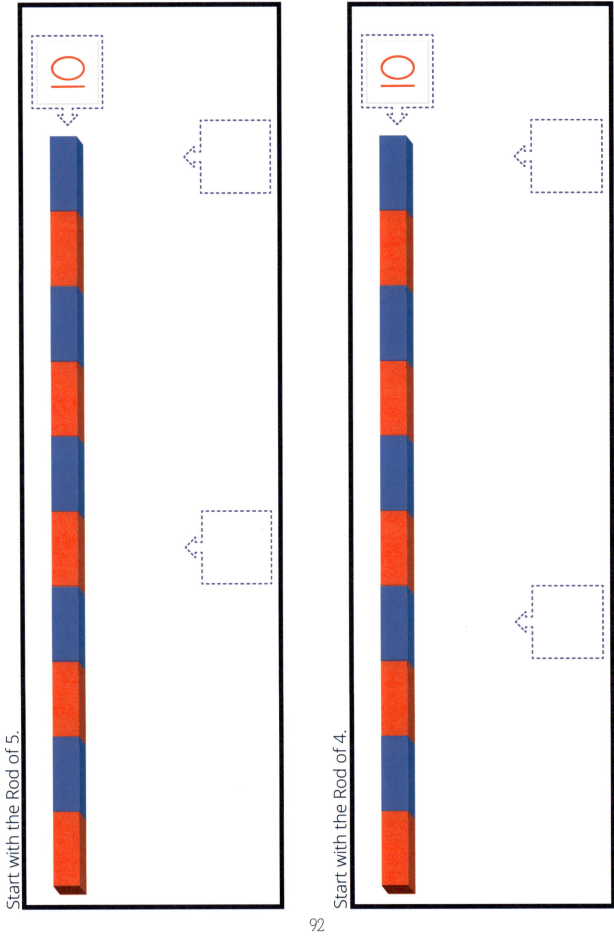

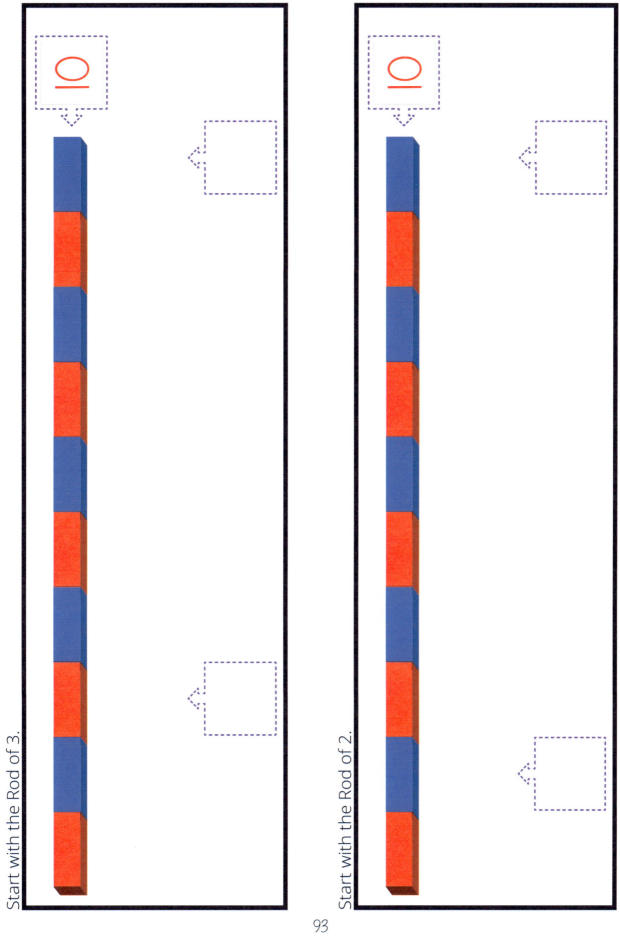

Start with the Rod of 3.

Start with the Rod of 2.

Start with the Rod of 1.

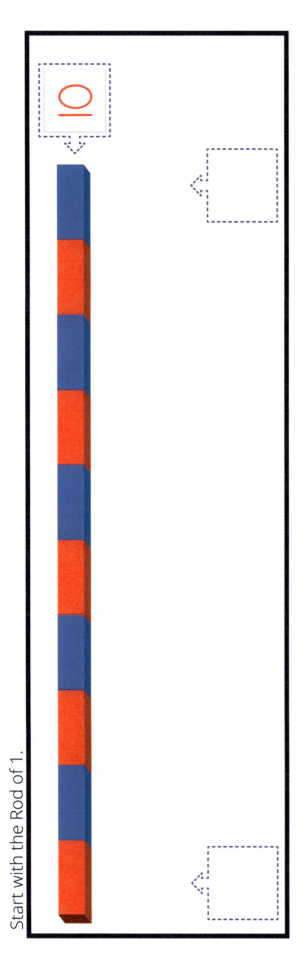

Number Rods and Cards: Subtract from Ten

This exercise is an initial exposure to subtraction, without writing number sentences. Follow the dialogue of the example problem for each subsequent problem. You will need to cut apart two sets of number rods 1-9 and two sets of number cards 1-9 for this lesson.

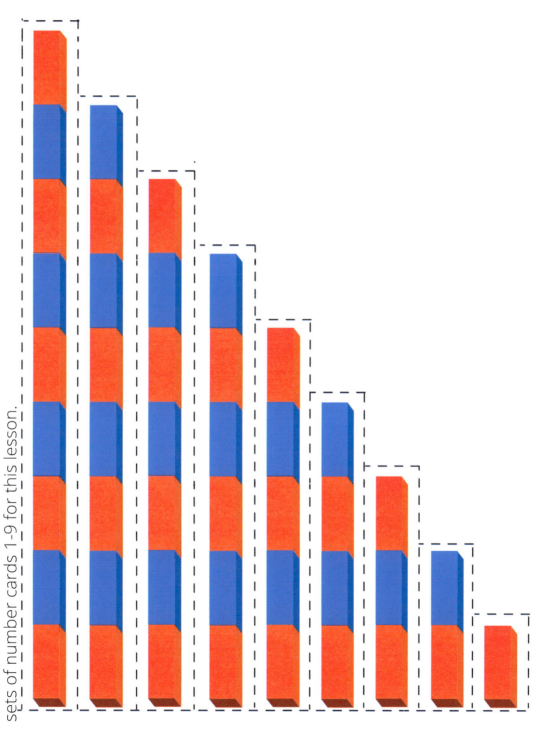

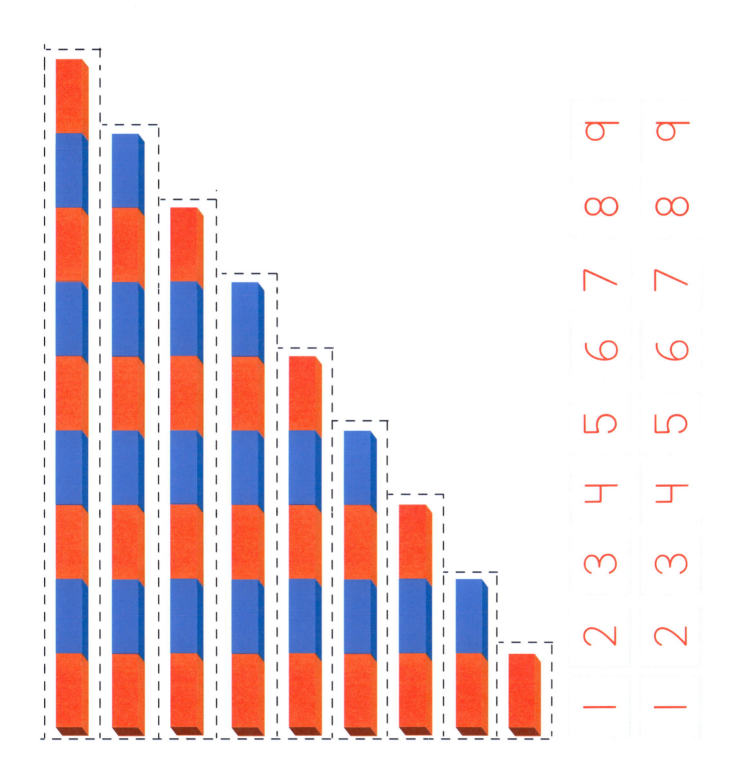

Number Rods and Cards: Subtract from Ten

Follow this Example: Please place the Rod of 9 directly underneath the Rod of 10. [Wait.]
Now place the "9" Numeral Card just underneath the last section of the Rod of 9. [Wait.]
Now, place the Rod of 1 directly to the right of the Rod of 9. [Wait.]
Now, place the "1" numeral card just underneath the Rod of 1. [Wait.]
Run your finger along the length of the rods as you say, "Nine plus one equals ten."
Run your finger the length of the bottom rods as you say, "Ten, take away one (remove Rod of 1) is nine."
Glue the Rod of 9 down, but do not glue the Rod of 1. Leave both number cards glued.

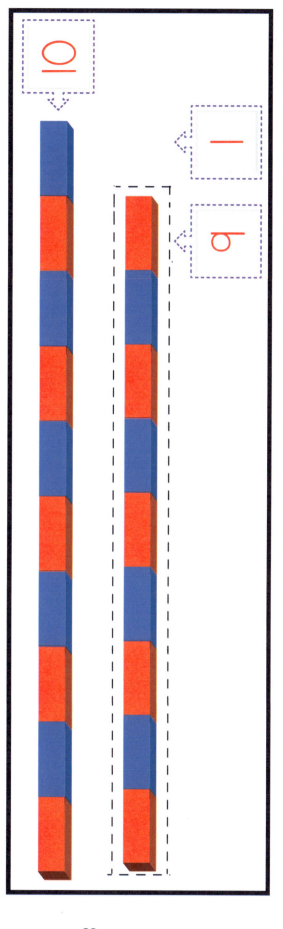

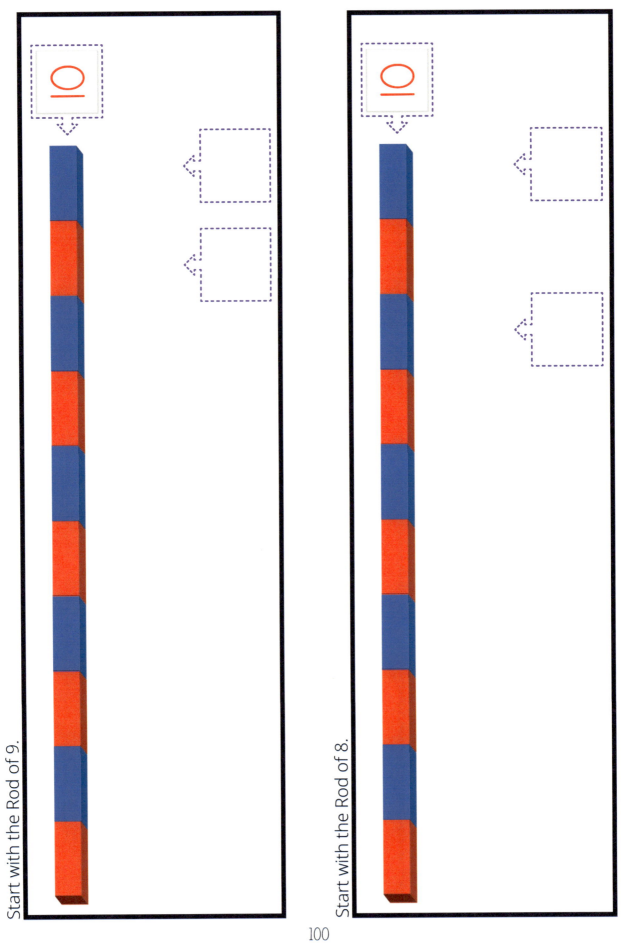

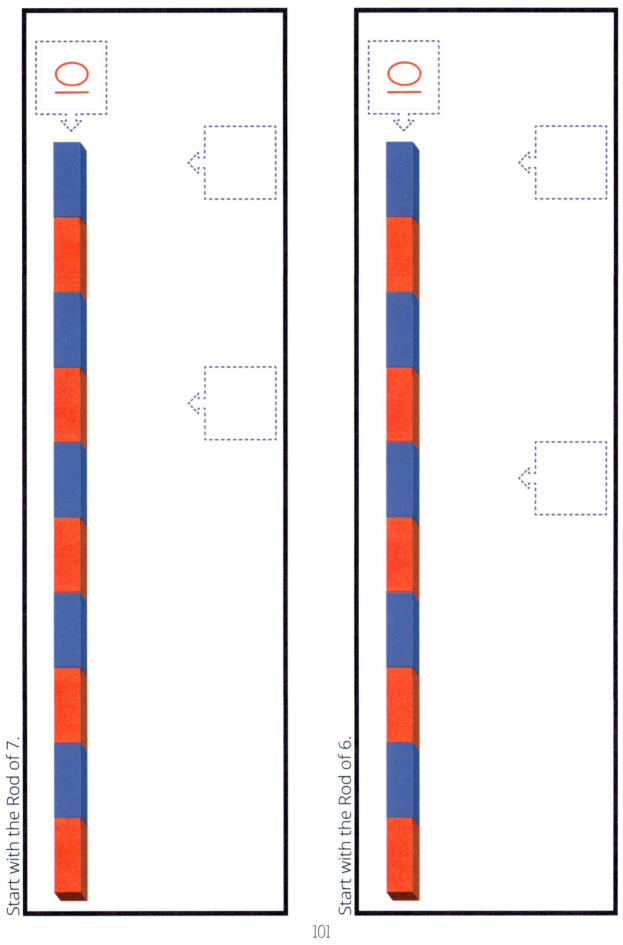

Start with the Rod of 7.

Start with the Rod of 6.

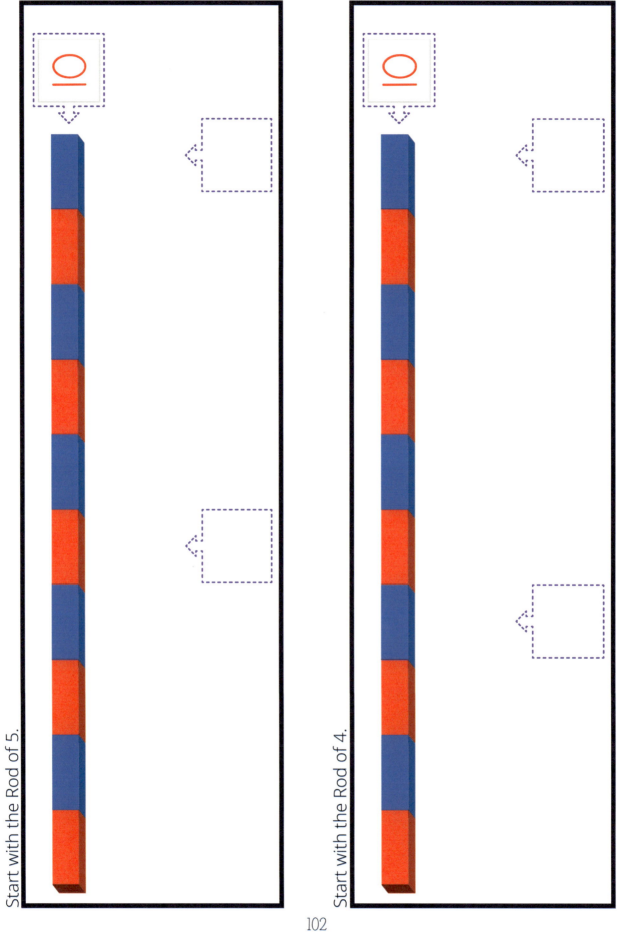

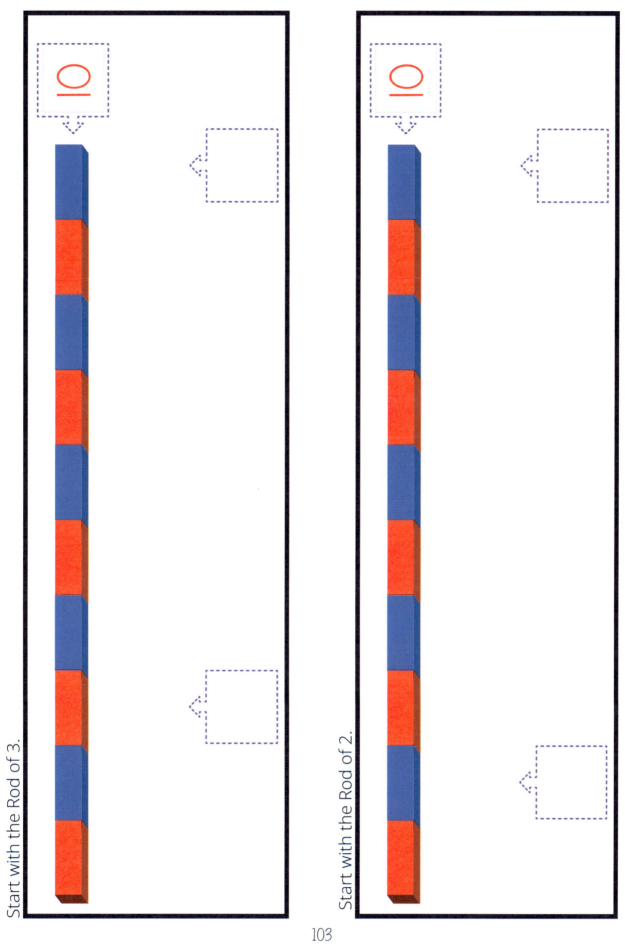

Start with the Rod of 3.

Start with the Rod of 2.

Start with the Rod of 1.

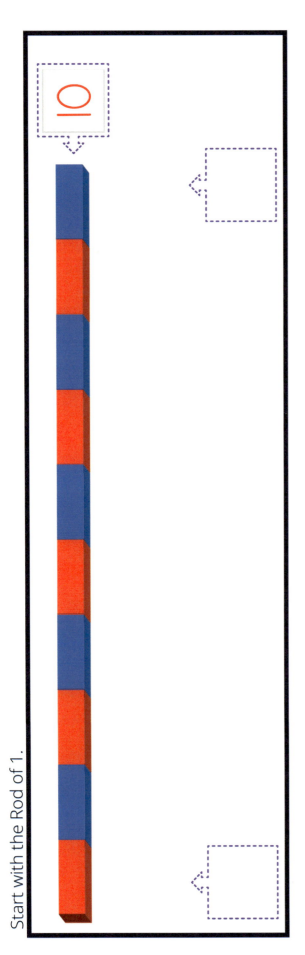

10

Cards and Counters

Directions: Count then color or use a dot marker for the counter underneath each number.

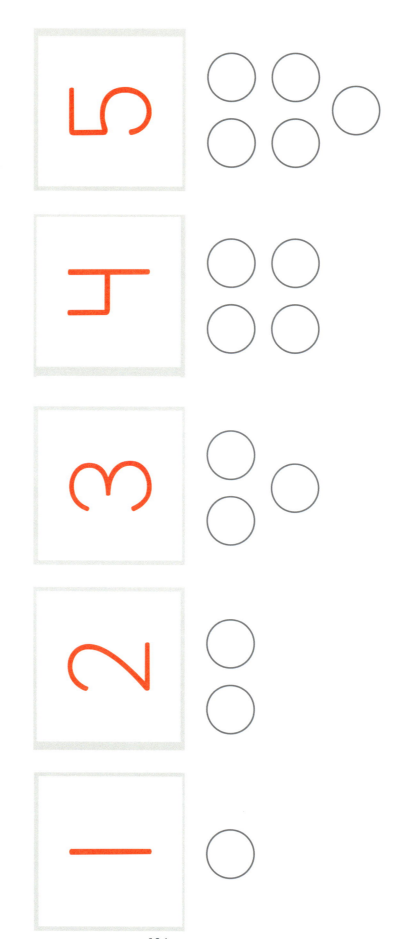

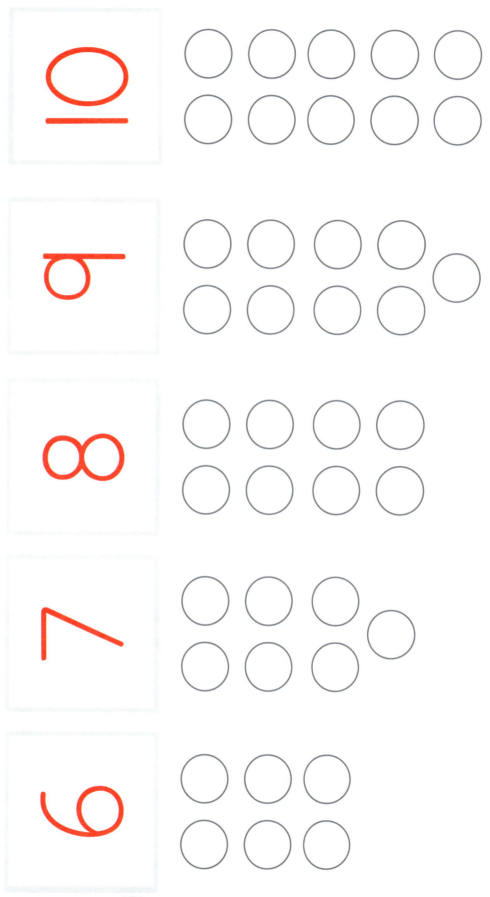

Cards and Counters: Identify the Number

Directions: Count the dots then mark the correct number by shading or circling it. Children who are writing can practice writing the number at the upper right hand corner of the box.

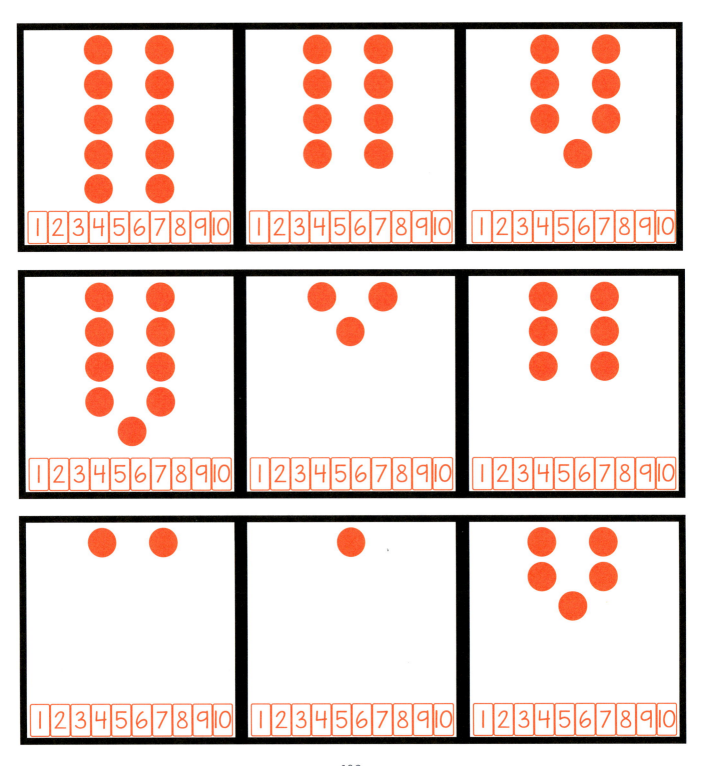

Cards and Counters: Dots and Numbers Match

Directions: Draw a line from the dots to the correct numeral.

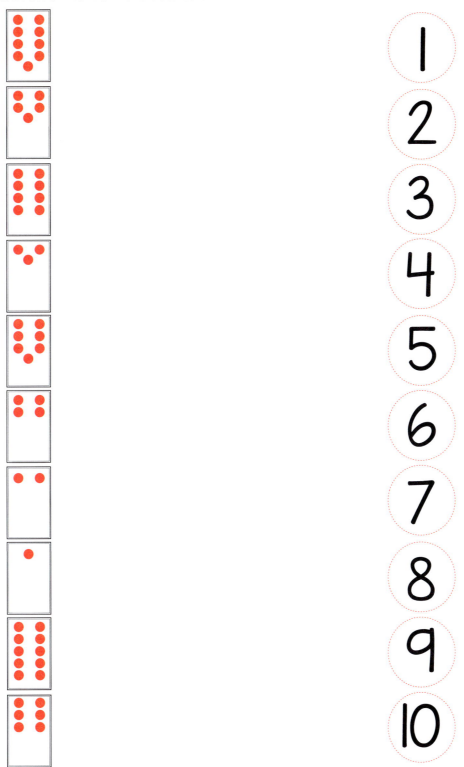

Cards and Counters: Dots and Numbers Match

Directions: Draw a line from the dots to the correct numeral.

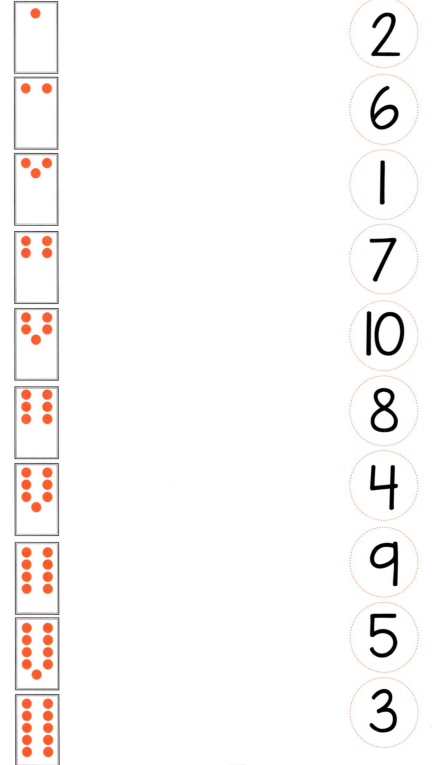

Cards and Counters: Even or Odd

Directions:
1. First invite your child to place the cards 1-10 in the gray boxes in order. The cards will cover the word "even" and the red up arrow. Ignore the odd and even words and arrows in the beginning.
2. After the cards are placed in order, add the counters (any 55 identical objects you may have*, or make them out of paper) as shown in the last exercises, pairing the counters and placing the "odd" counter by itself in the middle for the odd numbers and leaving a finger space between the paired counters.
3. Next, you are going to demonstrate "even" and "odd." When you get to the number 1, say, "This counter is all by itself. It is alone. It is not in a pair. This is an odd number." Run your finger from the bottom edge of the page up to the counter that is under the 1. Stop.
4. Go to the number 2. Count the counters. "One, two. These counters are in a pair. They are not alone. They are paired. Two is an even number." Run your finger from the bottom edge of the page up through the middle of the pair of counters (there should be no "odd" one in the middle to stop your finger.) When your finger reaches the card, push it up to the space above the gray box. It should now reveal the word "even" and the red arrow. Go back and read the word "odd" that points to the "1." And read the word "even" that points to the "2."
5. Continue in this manner for every card. When you are finished, your layout should look like the one below. Review all odd numbers and all even numbers separately.

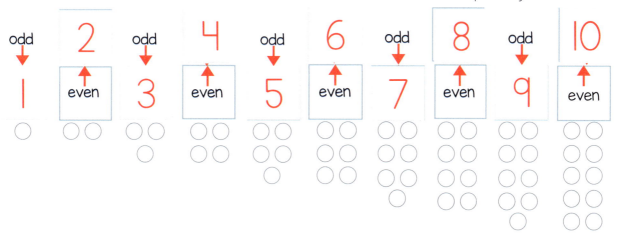

Cards and Counters: Even or Odd

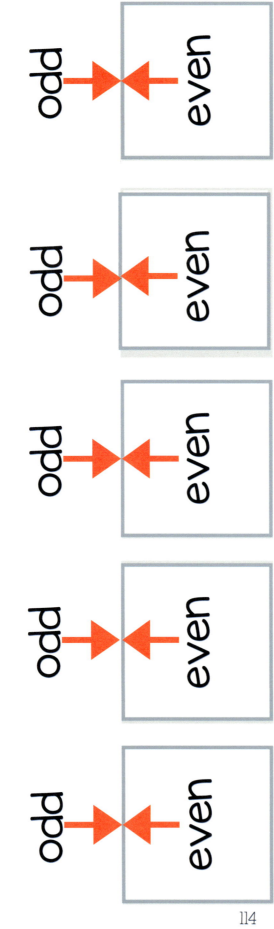

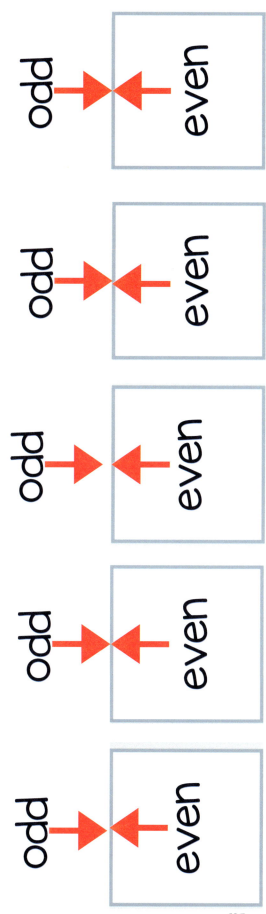

Cut these out for the
"Cards and Counters:
Even and Odd" Exercise.

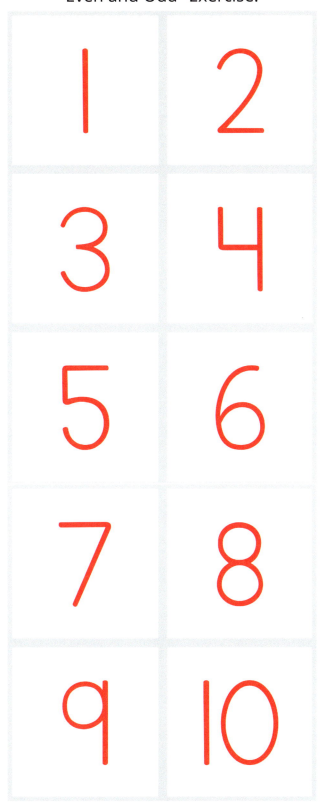

Cards and Counters: Even or Odd Exercise

Directions: Is there an even or odd amount of counters? Circle "even" or "odd."

even odd	even odd	even odd
even odd	even odd	even odd
even odd	even odd	even odd

Cards and Counters: Even or Odd Exercise

Directions: Is the number even or odd? Use physical counters or draw dots to check. Circle "even" or "odd."

5	2	4
even odd	even odd	even odd
6	7	9
even odd	even odd	even odd
1	3	8
even odd	even odd	even odd

Short Bead Bars: Intro

Directions:
Cut out a set of bead bars (**not** the ones on this page, as these are for a "control.) Place the cut out bead bars inside the triangle on the next page as you introduce each bar so it looks like the bead bars on this page. Start with 1. Say, "This is one." With two, say, "This is two." Then point and count, "One, two." Continue for all bead bars 1-9.

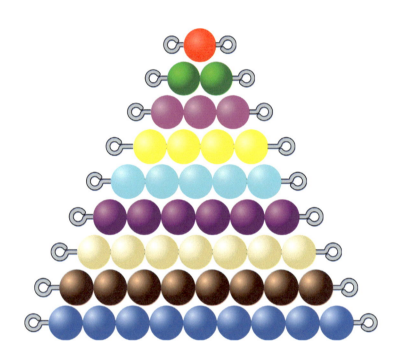

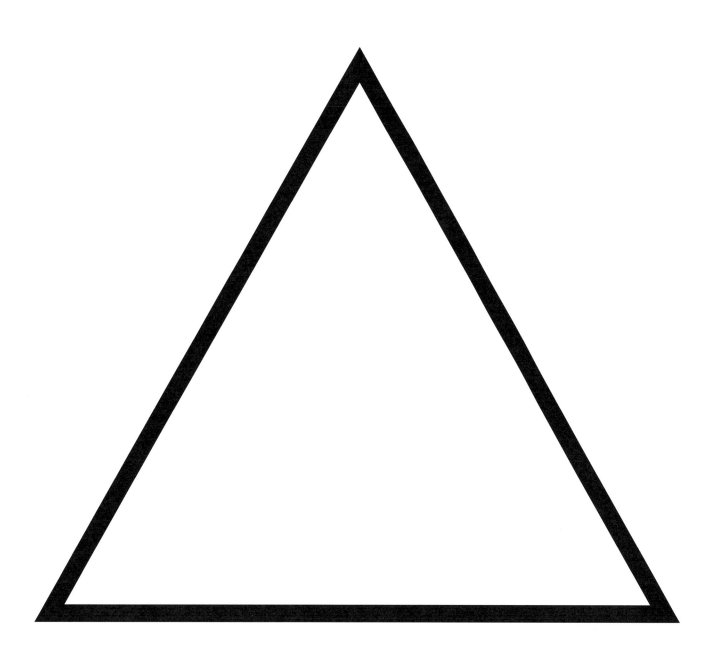

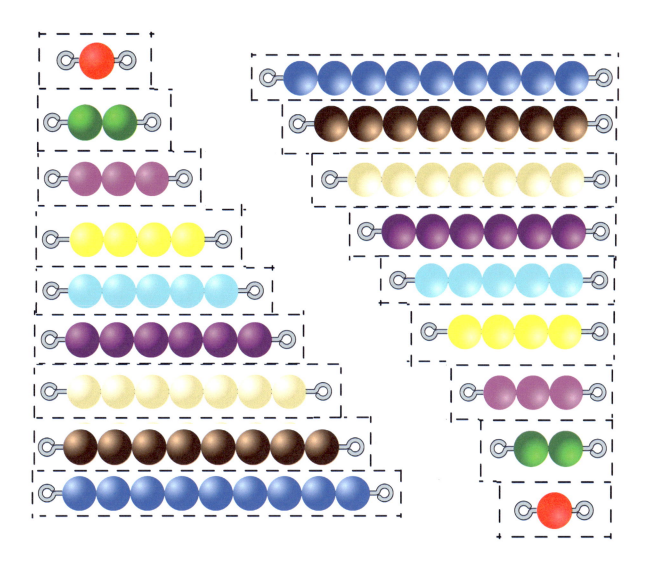

Short Bead Bars: Cut and Paste

Directions:
Invite your child to cut apart the bead bars and paste them in a pyramid, in order, in the tryiangle below. This will look just like the initial presentation you gave your child.

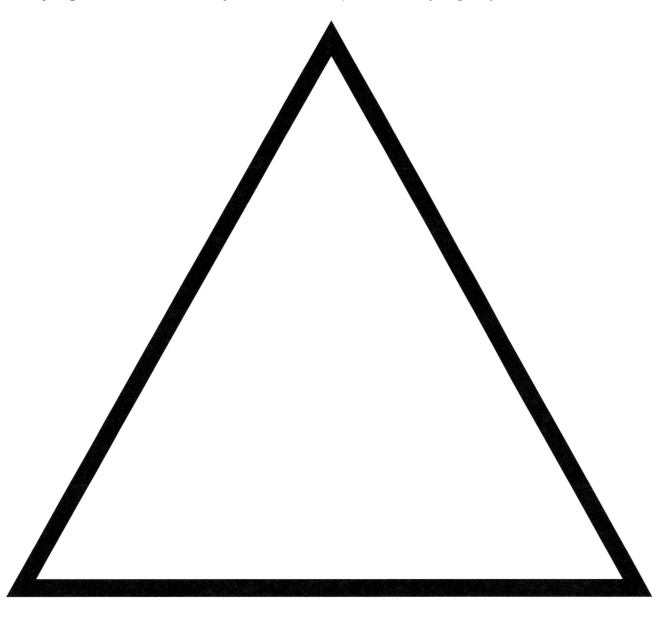

Short Bead Bars: Coloring the Stair

Directions:
Using the Bead Bar Cut and Paste as a Control for the colors, invite your cihild to color this bead stair.

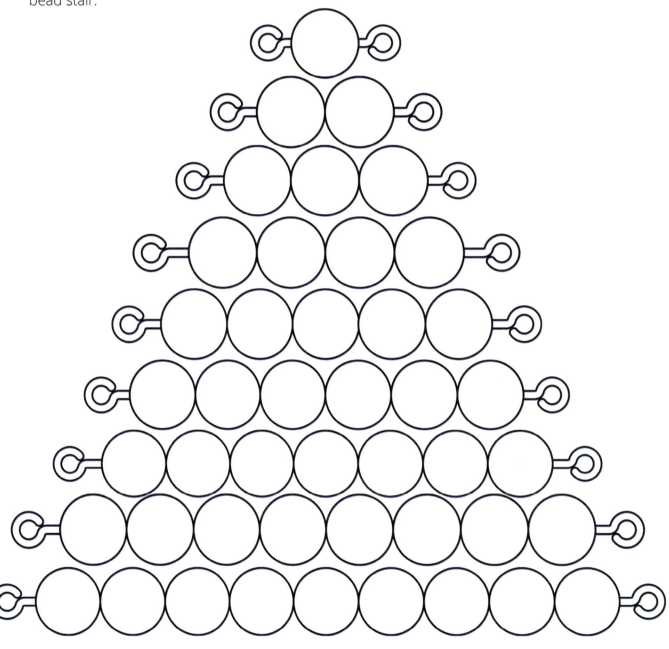

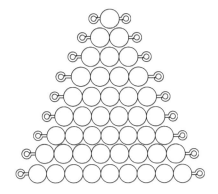

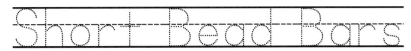

by:

raisingkingdomwarriors.com

   1

raisingkingdomwarriors.com

   2

raisingkingdomwarriors.com

raisingkingdomwarriors.com

Directions: Print and cut along the lines. Color the bead bars the same colors as the Montessori Bead Bars. (1 = red, 2 = green, 3 = pink, 4 = yellow, 5 = light blue, 6 = purple, 7 = white, 8 = brown, 9 = dark blue, 10 = gold.) Staple together to make a booklet.
IMPORTANT IF USING 1-10, use last page cover. IF USING 1-9, use first page cover and leave out the "10" page.

© 2019, raisingkingdomwarriors.com
Bead images by Bee Creative Clip Arts

 4

 5

 6

 7

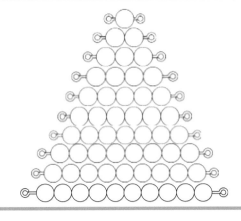 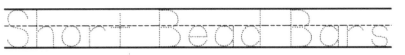

Number Match Game

Directions: Prep the number-bead cards by cutting off the number from the top of each card. You can use a specific cut pattern unique to each card as a control of error (variations of rounded and sharp cuts so the top will fit to the bottom like a puzzle.) There is a section for writing the number. If your child is not writing yet, you can use the numerals on this page to cut and paste.

Gather: Pre-cut number-bead cards, a set of short bead bars to cut, the numeral cards on this page if your child is not writing, and something to "make" the number.

Options for making the number: stamps (your child will stamp the same number of times), stickers, play dough, a dish of washable paint to dip a physical bead bar in and stamp it onto the page, or your child can write the name of the number with help.

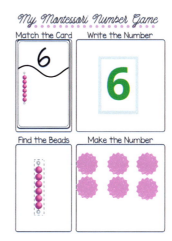

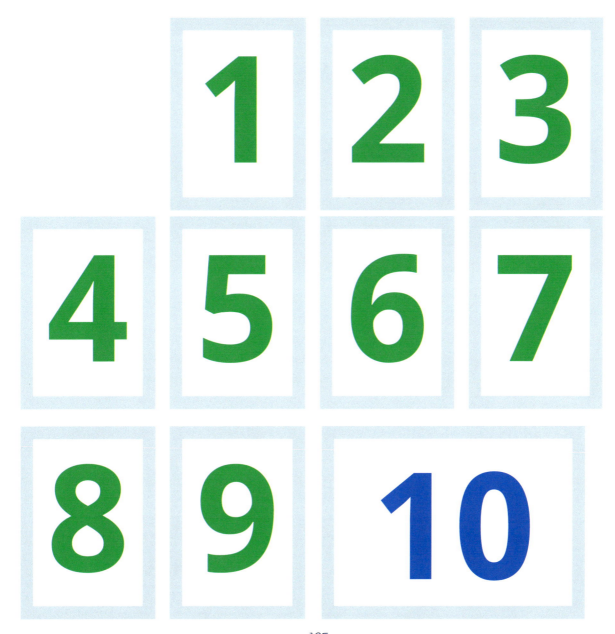

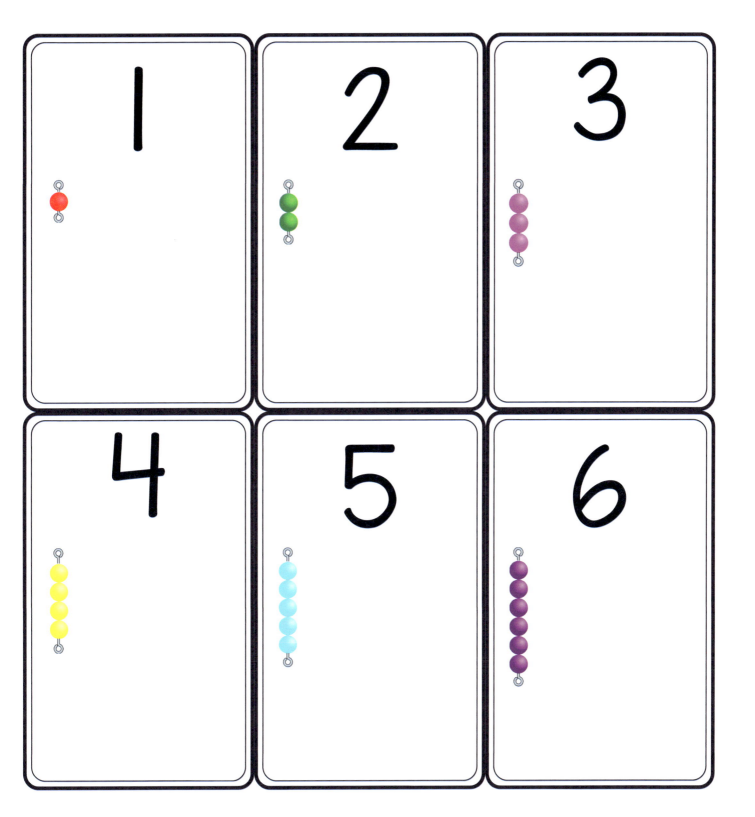

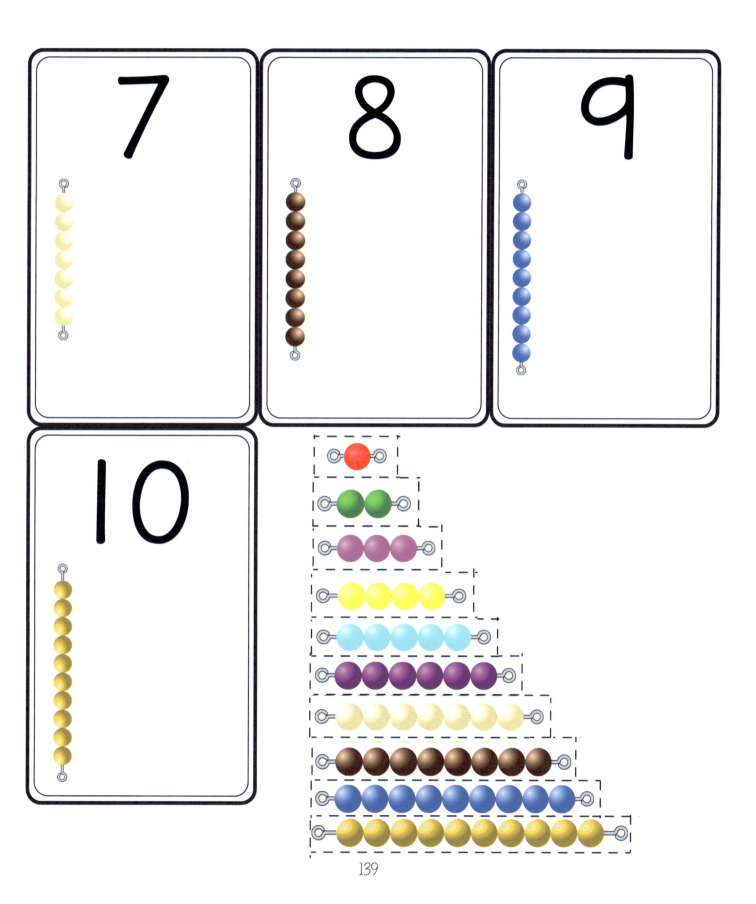

My Montessori Number Game

Match the Card

Write the Number

Find the Beads

Make the Number

My Montessori Number Game

Match the Card

Write the Number

Find the Beads

Make the Number

My Montessori Number Game

Match the Card

Write the Number

Find the Beads

Make the Number

My Montessori Number Game

Match the Card

Write the Number

Find the Beads

Make the Number

My Montessori Number Game

Match the Card

Write the Number

Find the Beads

Make the Number

My Montessori Number Game

Match the Card

Write the Number

Find the Beads

Make the Number

My Montessori Number Game

Match the Card

Write the Number

Find the Beads

Make the Number

My Montessori Number Game

Match the Card

Write the Number

Find the Beads

Make the Number

My Montessori Number Game

Match the Card

Write the Number

Find the Beads

Make the Number

My Montessori Number Game

Match the Card

Write the Number

Find the Beads

Make the Number

Bead Stairs for Activities

Use 1 bead stair for "Give the Beads by Name" and 1 or 3 bead stairs for "Short Bead Bars Design Cards." Depending on the amount of time you have for the math activities and your child's cutting ability, you can decide whether to pre-cut these or invite your child to cut them.

Give the Beads by Name

Directions: Cut out a set of short bead bars. Parent reads the prompts in the box. You will ask for each bead bar out of order. Your child will count aloud to verify the number is correct. Glue the bead bar into the box.

Please give me seven.

Please give me four.

Please give me one.

Please give me ten.

Please give me three.

> Please give me two.

> Please give me six.

> Please give me five.

> Please give me nine.

> Please give me eight.

Beads to Number

Directions: Invite your child to match the beads that are in order on the left to the numbers that are not in order on the right by drawing a line to connect the matches.

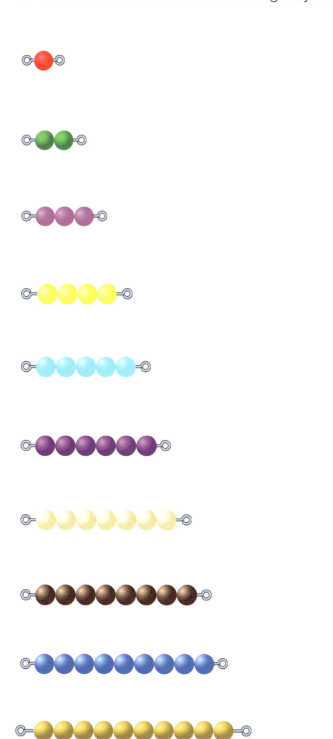

Number to Beads

Directions: Invite your child to match the numerals that are in order on the left to the beads that are not in order on the right by drawing a line to connect the matches.

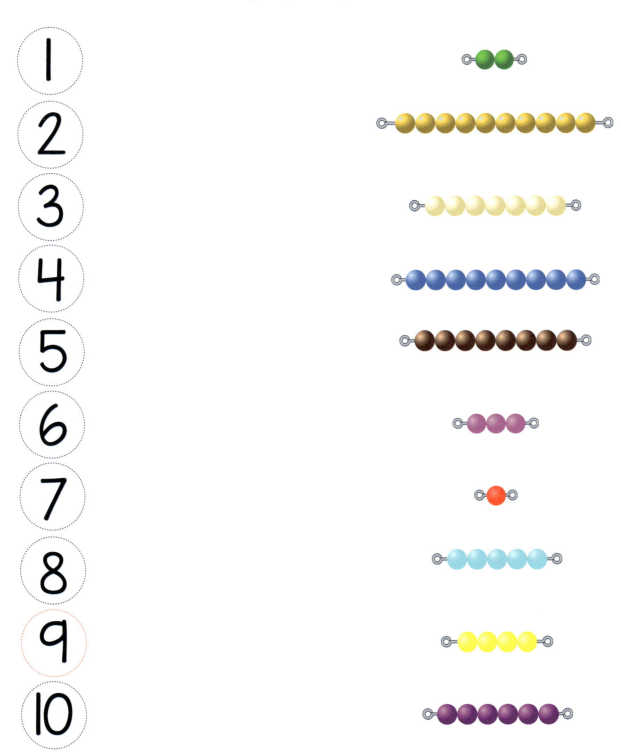

Bead Bars: Mixed Order to Mixed Order

Directions: Invite your child to match the numerals that are out of order on the left to the beads that are out of order on the right by drawing a line from the numeral to the matching bead bar.

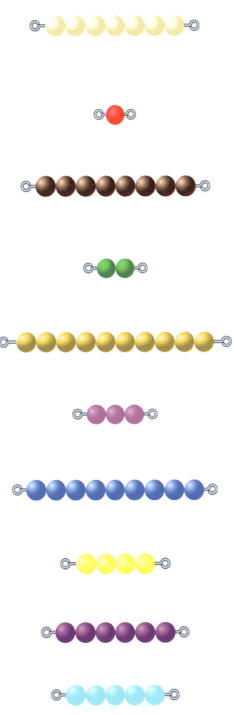

Short Bead Bars Design Cards

Directions: Cut out a set of short bead bars (or three sets if you want to glue them down.) Invite your child to copy the pattern into the box below. Invite your child the full "chain" or "snake" with you starting from the left hand side. The parent can write the full number to the bottom right of the box, if you desire.

*Note: You may need to use a blank sheet of paper to cover up the problems below the one your child is working on to isolate one pattern at a time.

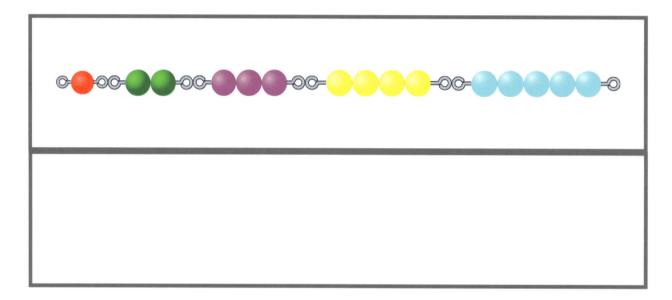

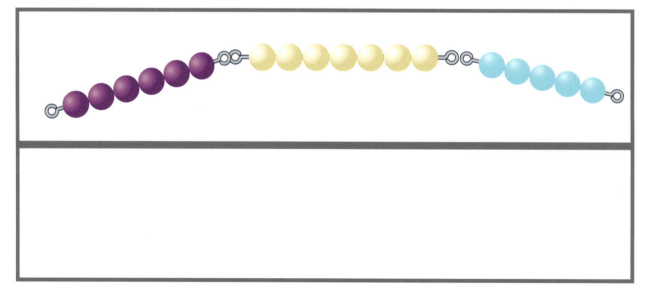

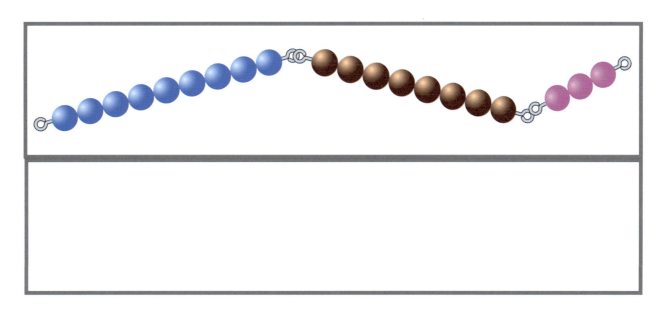

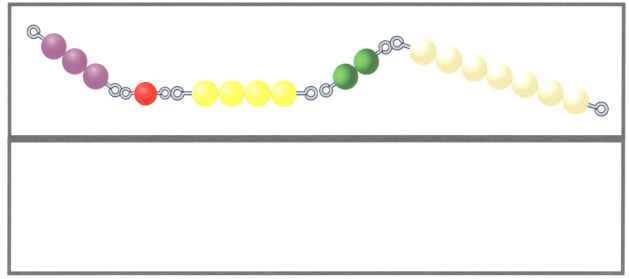

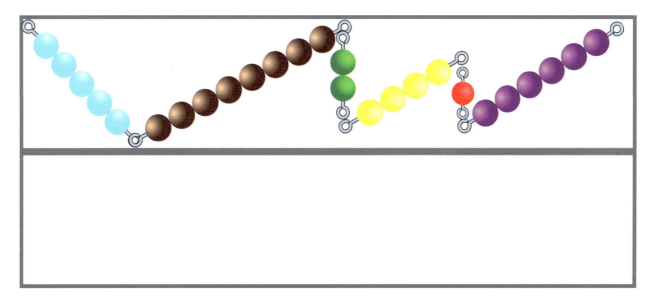

Make Ten Snake Game

Preparation:
1. Cut out three sets of short bead bars 1-9, 15 golden bead ten-bars, and one black and white bead stair.
2. The goal of this "game" is to turn a colored snake into a golden snake by counting to ten. For this first game, you will **not use the black and white bead bars**. Keep them visible, but tell your child you will not use them until the next game.
3. You will need the pre-cut beads (see #1), a pencil, and glue for this activity. Place the pre-cut bead bars onto the bead organizer and the black and white bead bars into a pyramid.

Directions:
1. First, "copy" the bead snake into the box below using your cut out bead bars. **Do not glue down the colored bead bars**.
2. Starting at the first bead on the left, count until you get to ten.
3. When you get to ten, stop and place a pencil mark at the end of the tenth bead.
4. Remove the colored bead bars and replace them with one golden bead ten-bar. Place the colored beads to the right of the work space in a separate pile. *You will use these again at the end to check the problem, so do not mix them with other beads.
5. Continue counting from the pencil mark until you get to ten again. Make a pencil mark to the right of the tenth bead.
6. Remove the colored beads, place them in your special pile from this problem, and replace those colored beads with another golden bead ten-bar.
7. Continue until the end of the snake. When you are done, say, "I have turned my colored snake into a golden snake by grouping the tens."
8. Lastly, check your work. Line up the golden beads in a straight, horizontal line. Then line up the reserved pile of colored beads from your original colored snake. Make sure they align bead under bead, which means the colored beads will either overlap or be staggered. Count each of them. Point to the colored snake and say, "this is ___(30, for example.)" Point to the golden snake and say, "This is ___ (30.)"
9. Glue down the golden snake. You can re-use the colored bead bars.

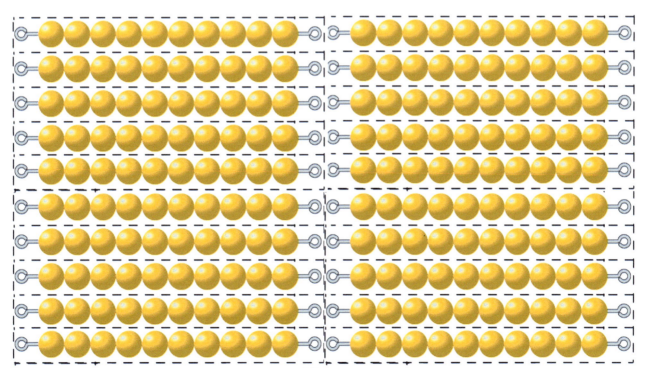

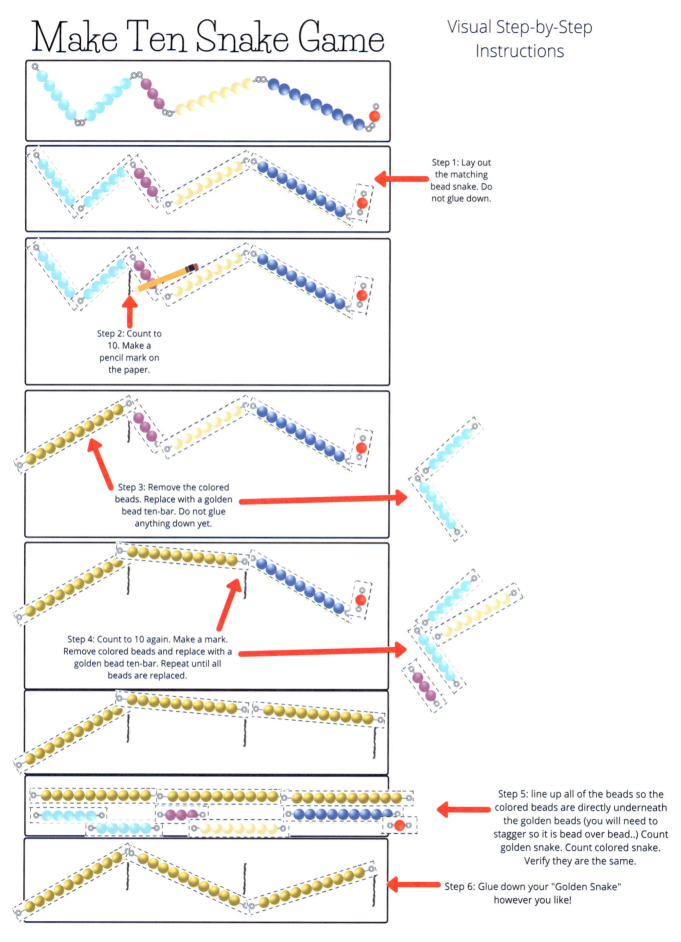

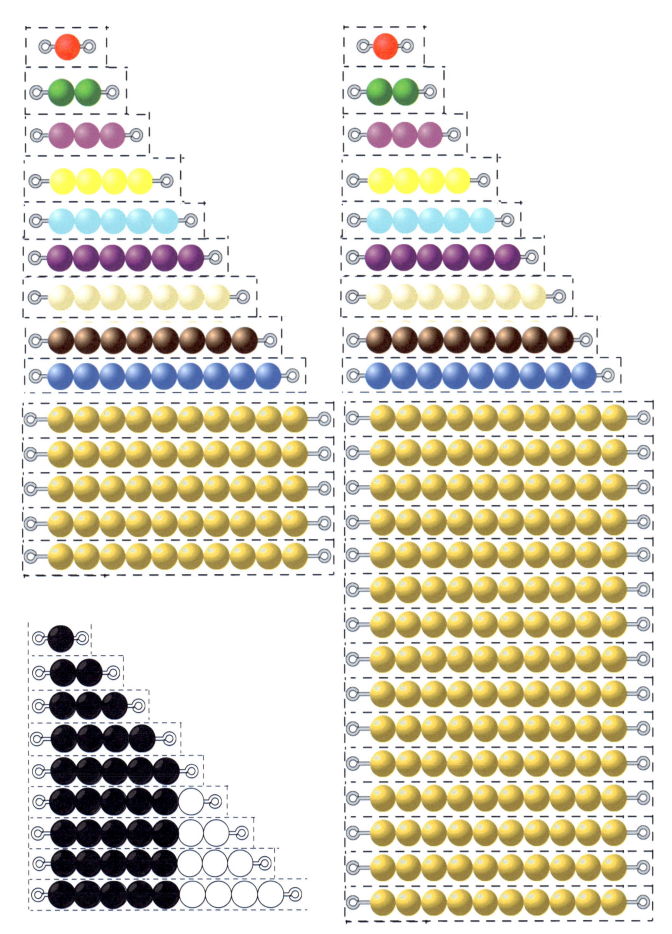

Bead Organizer

Use this organizer next to your workbook to organize your beads when working with the bead bars!

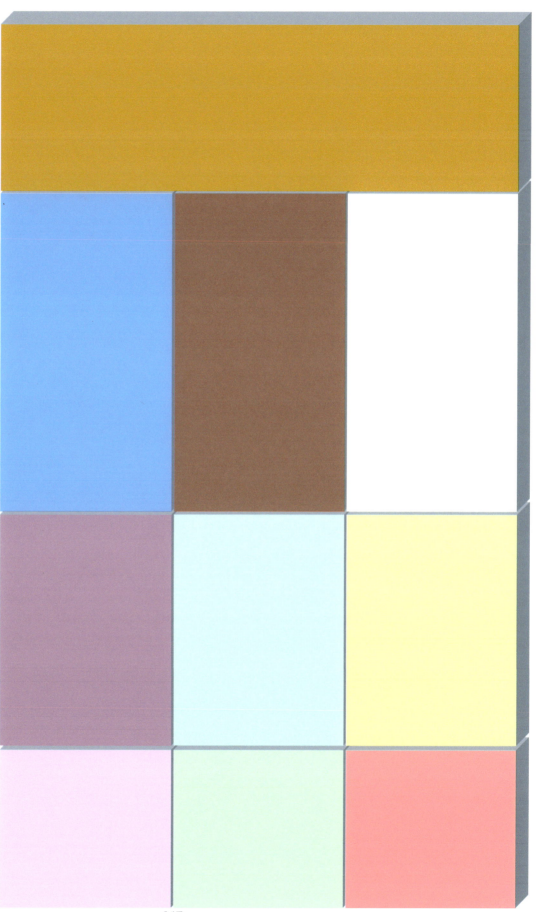

Make Ten Snake Game

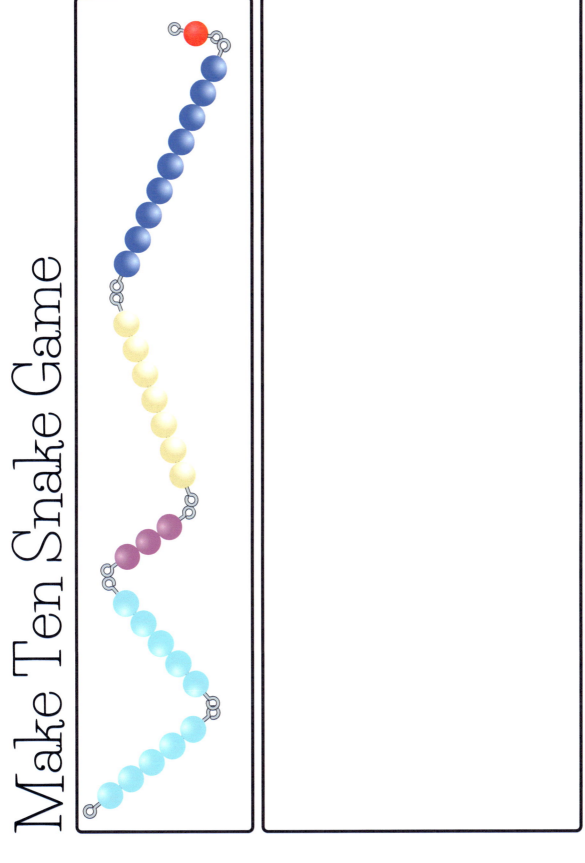

Make Ten Snake Game

Make Ten Snake Game

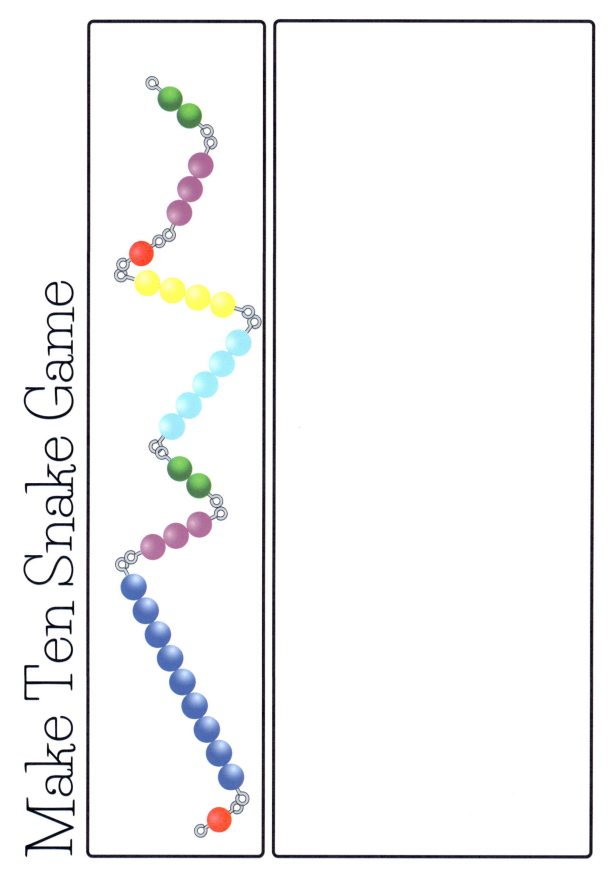

Make Ten Snake Game

Make Ten Snake Game

Make Ten Snake Game - Make Your Own Snake

Using the colored bead bars, make your own snakes for your child, making sure to build the snake in even groups of ten. You can re-use this mat again and again. Your child can use a "pointer" to hold the space instead of a pencil mark on the paper.

Make Ten Snake Game with the Black and White Bead Bars

Preparation:
1. Cut out three sets of short bead bars 1-9, 15 golden bead ten-bars, and one black and white bead stair.
2. The goal of this "game" is to turn a colored snake into a golden snake by counting to ten. For this first game, you **will use the black and white bead bars**.
3. You will need the pre-cut beads (see #1), a pencil, and glue for this activity. Place the pre-cut bead bars onto the bead organizer and the black and white bead bars into a pyramid.
4. Directions:

Directions:
1. First, "copy" the bead snake into the box below using your cut out bead bars. **Do not glue down the colored bead bars**.
2. Starting at the first bead on the left, count until you get to ten.
3. When you get to ten, stop and place a pencil mark at the end of the tenth bead.
4. If you stop in the middle of a bead bar, you also need to count the remaining beads to the right of your pencil mark.
5. Place a golden bead ten-bar above the ten colored beads and a black and white bead bar above the "remaining" beads if you stopped in the middle of a colored bead bar when counting to ten.
6. Remove the colored bead bars and replace them with one golden bead ten-bar and the black and white bead bar, if needed. Place the colored beads to the right of the work space in a separate pile. *You will use these again at the end to check the problem, so do not mix them with other beads.
7. Continue counting from the pencil mark, which will also be the first bead on the black and white bead bar, until you get to ten again. Make a pencil mark to the right of the tenth bead.
8. Remove the colored beads, place them in your special pile from this problem, and replace those colored beads with another golden bead ten-bar and the proper black and white bead bar, if needed.
9. Continue until the end of the snake. Use a black and white bead bar for the end of the snake, if you don't have an even ten. When you are done, say, "I have turned my colored snake into a golden snake with a black and white tail by grouping the tens."
10. Lastly, check your work. Line up the golden beads (and black and white tail) in a straight, horizontal line. Then line up the reserved pile of colored beads from your original colored snake. Make sure they align bead under bead, which means the colored beads will either overlap or be staggered. Count each of them. Point to the colored snake and say, "this is ___(31, for example.)" Point to the golden snake and say, "This is ___ (31.)"
11. Glue down the golden snake. Draw the black and white tail with a pencil. You can re-use the colored bead bars and black and white bead bars.

Make Ten Snake Game

Visual Step-by-Step Instructions

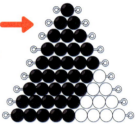

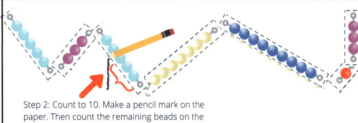

Step 1: Lay out the matching bead snake. Do not glue down. Place black and white beads in a pyramid by your work space.

Step 2: Count to 10. Make a pencil mark on the paper. Then count the remaining beads on the bead bar if you stop in the middle of a bead bar.

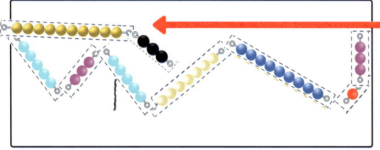

Step 3: Place the Golden Bead Ten-Bar above the ten colored beads you just counted and a black and white bead bar above the "remaining" beads on the colored bead bar that you stopped in the middle of when counting to ten.

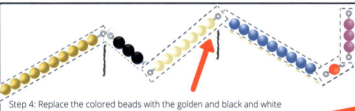

Step 4: Replace the colored beads with the golden and black and white beads. Place the colored beads off to the side in a reserved pile. Then count to ten again starting from the pencil mark and first black and white bead. Make another pencil mark at ten more beads.

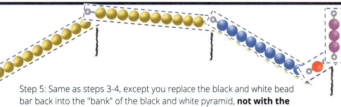

Step 5: Same as steps 3-4, except you replace the black and white bead bar back into the "bank" of the black and white pyramid, **not with the colored bead bar pile.**

Step 5: line up all of the beads so the colored beads are directly underneath the golden beads (you will need to stagger so it is bead over bead..) Count golden snake with black/white tail. Count colored snake. Verify they are the same.

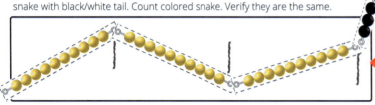

Step 6: Glue down your "Golden Snake" however you like! Then draw on the black and white tail. Replace the black and white bead bar to the pyramid.

176

Make Ten Snake Game - Random

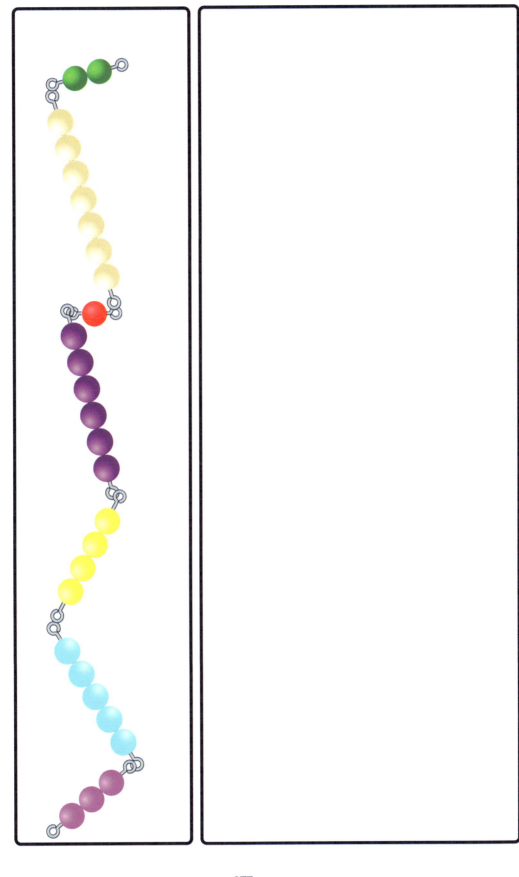

Make Ten Snake Game - Random

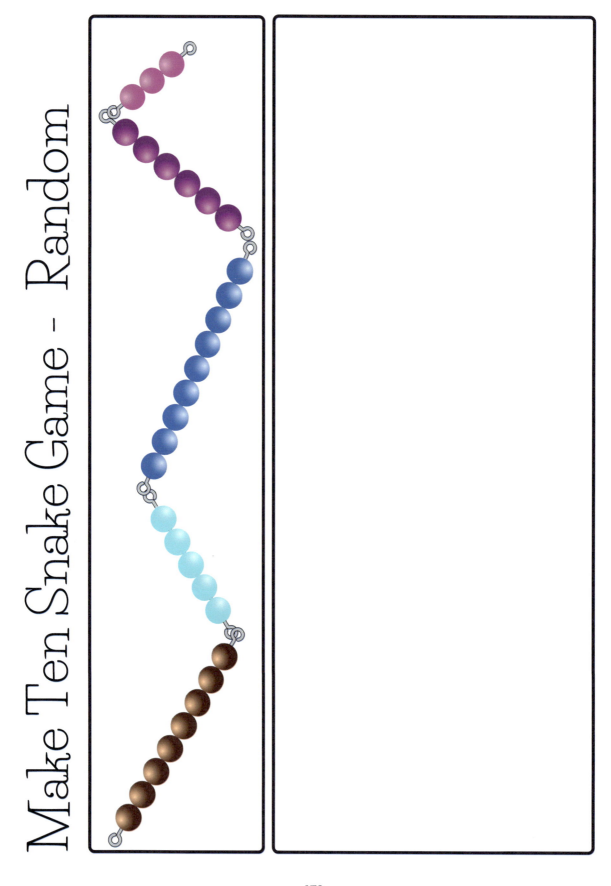

Make Ten Snake Game - Random

Make Ten Snake Game - Random

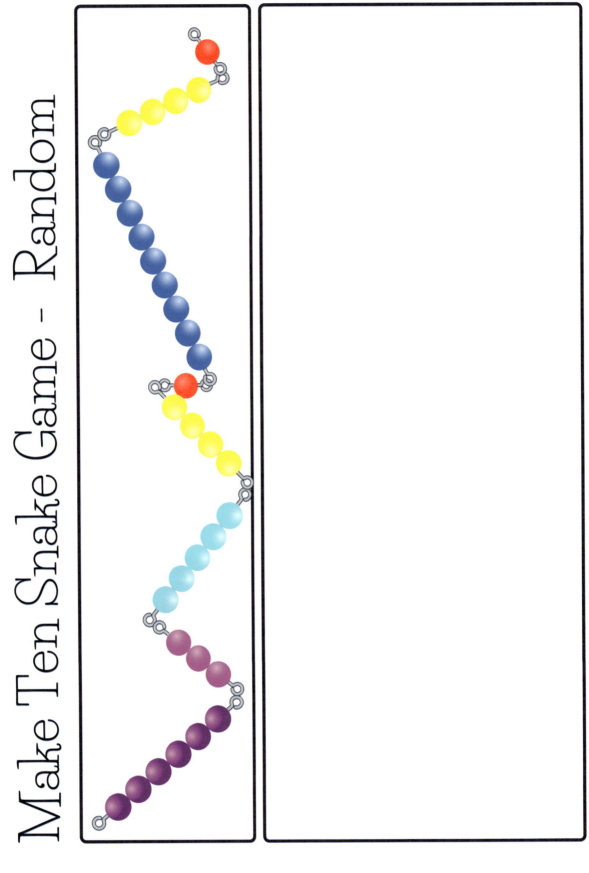

Make Ten Snake Game - Random

Make Ten Snake Game - Child-Made Random Snake

Using the colored bead bars, invite your child to make his or her own snake. You can re-use this mat again and again. Your child can use a "pointer" to hold the space instead of a pencil mark on the paper. Use the black and white bead bars as needed.

Introduction to Teen Values with Beads

This presentation will introduce your child to the *values* of the teen numbers before the written numerals. We will introduce three values at a time. Your child should be able to tell you the values of the amounts when asked (which is the second period in the three-period lesson) and make the amounts when asked (which is the third period.) This lesson is broken up into three parts: 11-13, 14-16, and 17-18. The directions for each lesson can be repeated the same way for each group of teen numbers.

Directions: Cut out 9 golden bead ten-bars and one set of colored beads 1-9 (both on the bottom of this page.)

Lesson 1:
1. Point to the ten-bar on the left hand side of the box and say "ten," then point to the colored bead and say "and one (its amount) equals eleven (the total)."
2. Next, build the number on the right, saying the exact same thing as you set down the beads.
3. Continue for 11-13. Leave the beads in the boxes.
4. Put the beads away.

Lesson 2:
1. Invite your child to make 11-13 the same way you showed in Lesson 1.
2. Put the beads away.

Lesson 3:
1. Cover the left hand column for all of the given amounts.
2. Invite your child to make 11-13 *without looking* at the key in the lefthand column.
3. Invite your child to check his or her work when finished. Repeat as many times as desired.

Lesson 4:
When your child has mastered the amounts, he or she can glue down the bead bars.

Note: Ideally, you will not move on to the next set of teen numbers (14-16 then 17-19) until your child has mastered the previous set.

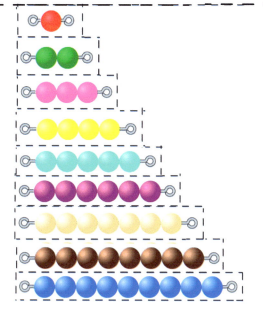
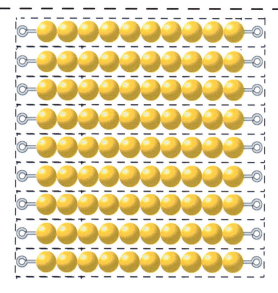

Introduction to Teen Values with Beads - Set 1

This is eleven. Ten (point to the ten-bar) and one (point to the one bead) is eleven.

This is twelve. Ten (point to the ten-bar) and two (point to the two-bar) is twelve.

This is thirteen. Ten (point to the ten-bar) and three (point to the three-bar) is thirteen.

Practicing 11-13 with Beads

You will play a series of games for today's activity to help your child retain a firm grasp on these amounts.

Directions:
1. Invite your child to cut out the bead cards for 11-13.
2. Say, "Please place these cards in order from left to right."
3. Say, "Show me 11." [Wait.] "Show me 12." [Wait] "Show me 13." [Wait.]
4. Mix up the cards and repeat #3.
5. Now flip the cards over, mix them up, and place them in a row.
6. Ask your child to flip over the first card and tell you the value. Leave it face-up. Continue for all three cards.
7. Shuffle the cards and repeat #5-6.
8. Using a set of cut-out beads, invite your child to make the quantities 11, 12, and 13. You do not need to glue these down.
9. Lastly, glue down the bead cards in order on this page.

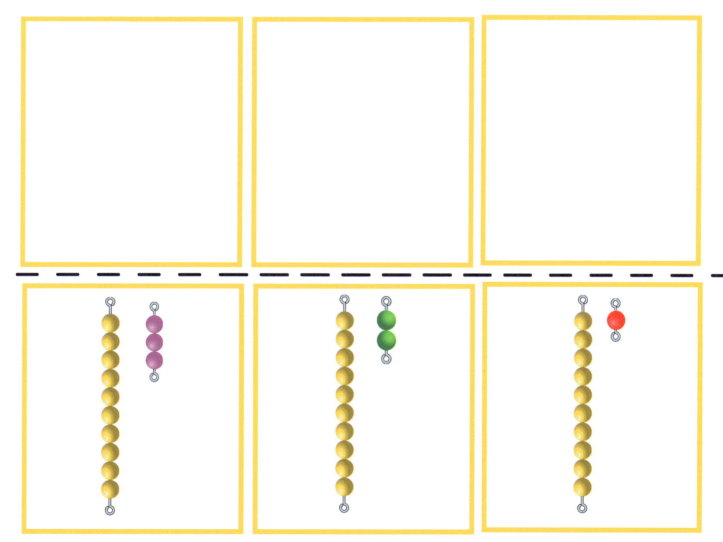

Introduction to Teen Values with Beads - Set 2

This is fourteen. Ten (point to the ten-bar) and four (point to the four-bar) is fourteen.

This is fifteen. Ten (point to the ten-bar) and five (point to the five-bar) is fifteen.

This is sixteen. Ten (point to the ten-bar) and six (point to the six-bar) is sixteen.

Practicing 14-16 with Beads

You will play a series of games for today's activity to help your child attain a firm grasp on these amounts.

Directions:
1. Invite your child to cut out the bead cards for 14-16.
2. Say, "Please place these cards in order from left to right."
3. Say, "Show me 14." [Wait.] "Show me 15." [Wait] "Show me 16." [Wait.]
4. Mix up the cards and repeat #3.
5. Now flip the cards over, mix them up, and place them in a row.
6. Ask your child to flip over the first card and tell you the value. Leave it face-up. Continue for all three cards.
7. Shuffle the cards and repeat #5-6.
8. Using a set of cut-out beads, invite your child to make the quantities 14, 15, and 16. You do not need to glue down the cut-out beads.
9. Lastly, glue down the bead cards in order on this page.

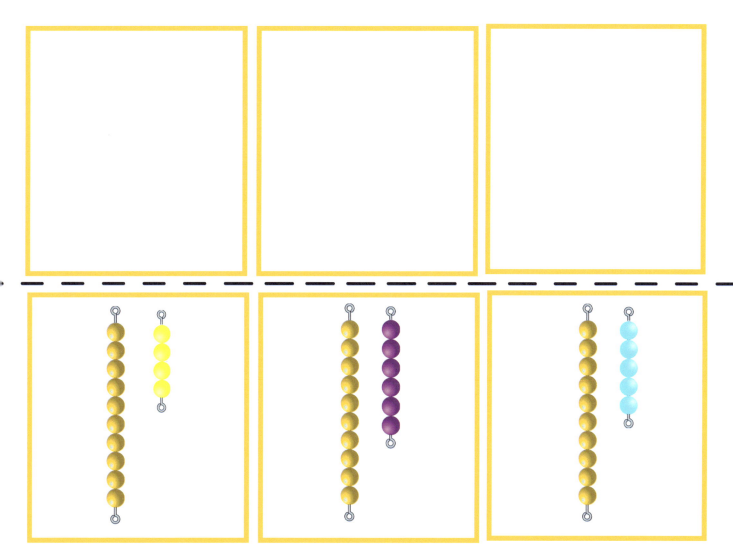

Introduction to Teen Values with Beads - Set 3

This is seventeen. Ten (point to the ten-bar) and four (point to the seven-bar) is seventeen.

This is eighteen. Ten (point to the ten-bar) and eight (point to the eight-bar) is eighteen.

This is nineteen. Ten (point to the ten-bar) and nine (point to the nine-bar) is nineteen.

Practicing 17-19 with Beads

You will play a series of games for today's activity to help your child retain a firm grasp on these amounts.
Directions:
1. Invite your child to cut out the bead cards for 17-19.
2. Say, "Please place these cards in order from left to right."
3. Say, "Show me 17." [Wait.] "Show me 18." [Wait] "Show me 19." [Wait.]
4. Mix up the cards and repeat #3.
5. Now flip the cards over, mix them up, and place them in a row face down.
6. Ask your child to flip over the first card and tell you the value. Leave it face-up. Continue for all three cards.
7. Shuffle the cards and repeat #5-6.
8. Using a set of cut-out beads, invite your child to make the quantities 17, 18, and 19. You do not need to glue these down.
9. Lastly, glue down the bead cards in order on this page.

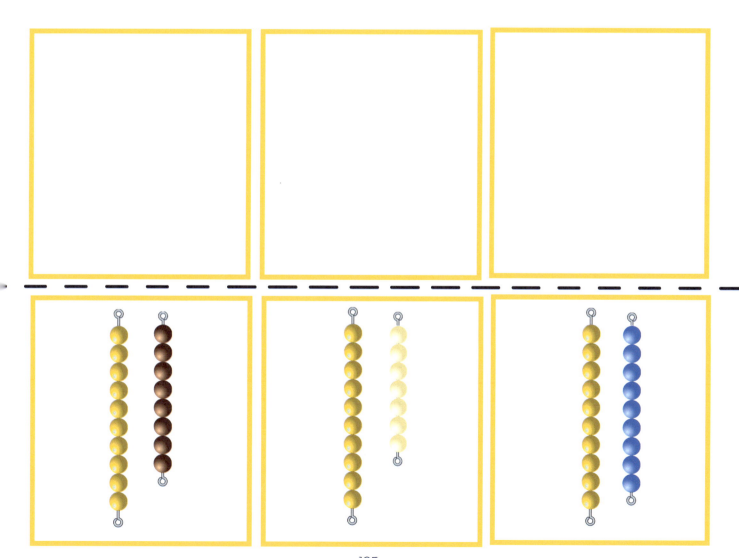

Beads for Teen Activities

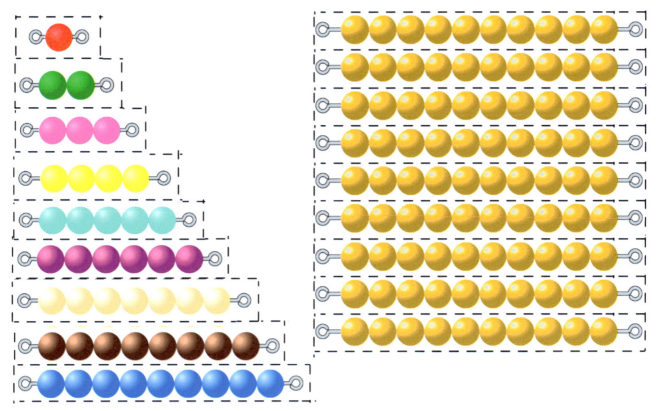

Top Half: "Teen Number Matching Game"

Bottom Half:
Set 1: "Teen Numerals - Introduction Using Teen Boards" (one colored bead stair and 9 ten-bars)
Set 2: "Teen Numbers - Teen Bead Hanger" (one colored bead stair and 9 ten-bars)

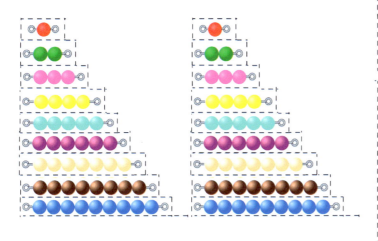
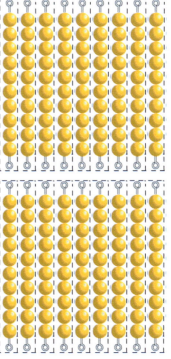

Teen Numerals – Introduction Using Teen Boards

First Lesson: Introduce the teen numerals **by themselves**. This will be a teaching lesson, where your child should watch you carefully. Pre-cut the numerals on this page 1-9, with the wood strips attached. Open up to the Teen Boards.

1. Lay out the numeral cards 1-9 vertically to the right of the open workbook.
2. Point to the first "10" and say, "Ten." Place the "1" on top of the "0" and say, "and one is eleven." Point to the "11" you just made and repeat, "eleven."
3. Continue for 11-19. Then take them off and invite your child to place the cards in their spots and say the numbers (if he is interested, it is not necessary to do right away.)

Second Lesson: Repeat the first lesson, but now you will also place the beads. (You need to lay out 9 ten-bars and a neat pyramid of one pre-cut colored bead stair 1-9.

1. Lay out the numeral cards 1-9 vertically to the right of the open workbook.
2. Point to the first "10" and say, "Ten." Place the "1" on top of the "0" and say, "and one is eleven." Point to the "11" you just made and repeat "eleven."
3. Take one ten-bar and place it vertically to the right of the 11 you just made. Point to the bar and say, "ten." Then place the one-bar and say, "and one is eleven."
4. Repeat for 11-19. Do not glue down.

Child's Activity: When your child is ready, invite him or her to place the cards and the cut-out beads in their spots on the ten boards (with beads placed vertically, to the right side). When everything is in its place, he or she can glue everything down. The numerals 1-9 can be glued on the top "wood" strip only so that they can be like "flaps" that can be opened, revealing the "10" underneath.

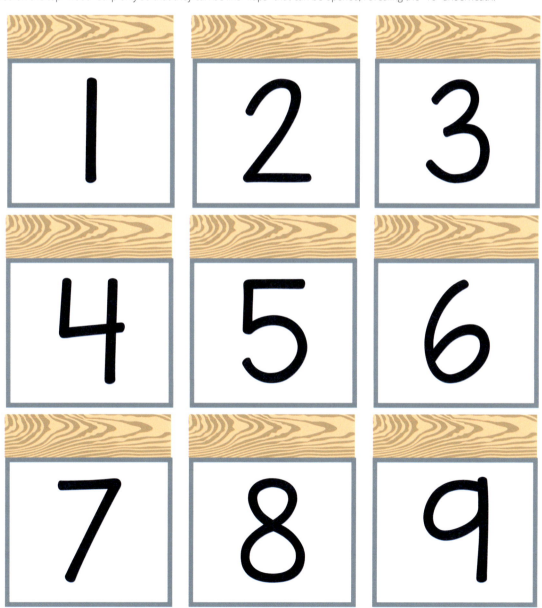

Teen Boards

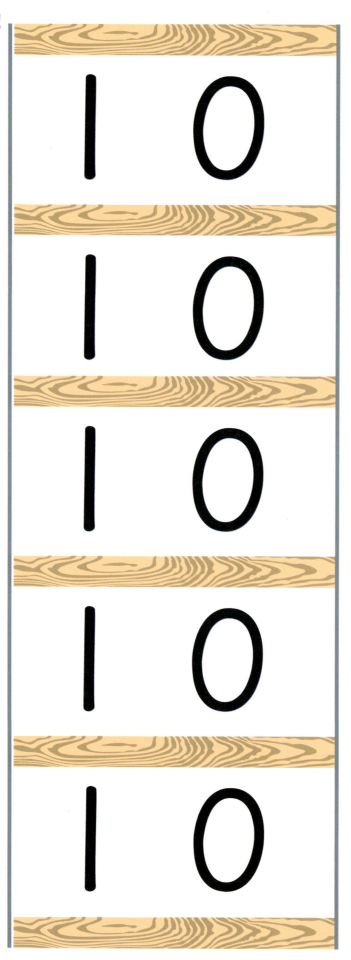

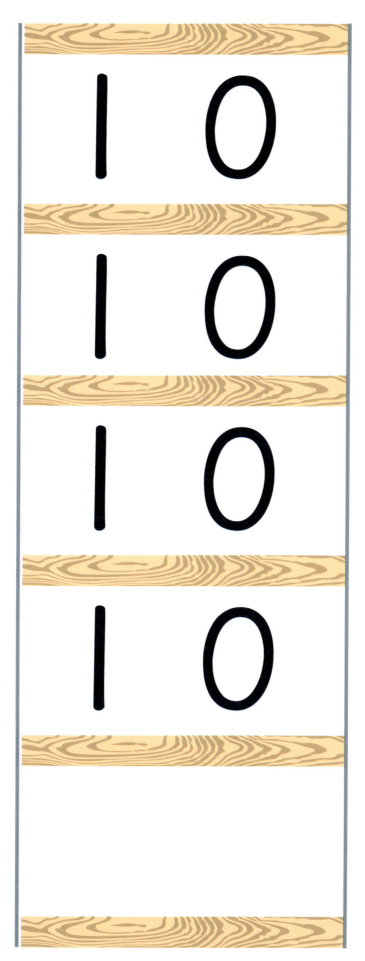

Teen Numbers - Teen Bead Hanger

The teen bead hanger is a beautiful math material found in many Montessori classrooms. It is an excellent visual for "seeing' the hanging beads, and the fine motor work required to hang the beads is a lesson in itself. We will replicate this activity on paper. I recommend that your child do all the cutting for this exercise. The beads will be on the smaller side to fit in the area of the hanger, and these "wooden" numeral tiles are small, as well.

Directions:
1. Cut the individual beads (9 ten-bars) and one each of 1-9.
2. Cut the "control ruler," making sure to keep the number cards all attached.
3. Cut the individual numeral tiles apart.
4. Place the nine golden bead ten-bars in the rectangular compartment on the hanger base.
5. Place the nine colored bead bars in the triangular compartment on the hanger base, aligning them in a pyramid shape in order, with the one-bar on the top.
6. Place the numeral tiles in mixed order below the paper hanger, in a horizontal line.
7. For the first time doing this activity, you may want to use the "control ruler" by placing it in the spot on the base of the hanger in the very back. If your child has been doing well with the other teen number activities, you may want to flip the control ruler face-down, and use it at the end when he is done placing the number tiles.
8. Show your child how to place the beads like he is "hanging" them. Go in order from 11-19. Place the ten bar on the left hook, "hanging down" and the colored bead to its right. Then place the corresponding numeral tile on the top bar. See the photo on this page of a completed teen hanger.
9. When all of the beads and tiles have been placed, invite your child to flip over the ruler and check his work.
10. NOTE: You may want to try some variations before inviting your child to glue everything in place. Or you may want to make several copies of this activity to try different variations.

Variations:
1. Do all the beads and then place the numeral tiles.
2. Do all the numeral tiles and then place the beads.
3. Choose one set of beads (for 16, for example) and invite your child to hang it in its place.
4. Choose one numeral tile and invite your child to place it in its spot.
5. Place one numeral or set of beads and ask your child to hang the beads and/or numeral that is "one more/less" or "two more/less."

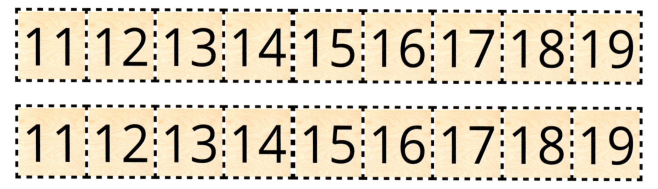

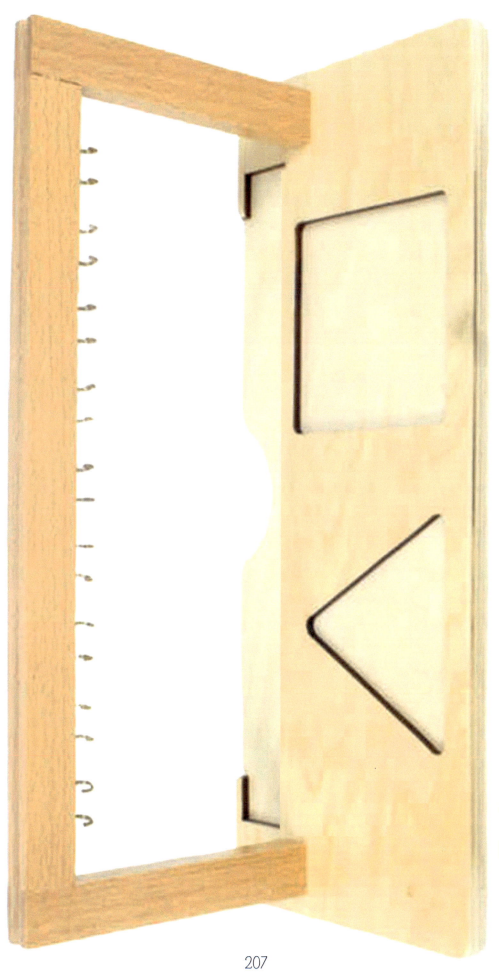

Teen Numbers - Numeral and Quantity Match

Order to mixed order. Draw a line from the number on the left to the matching beads on the right.

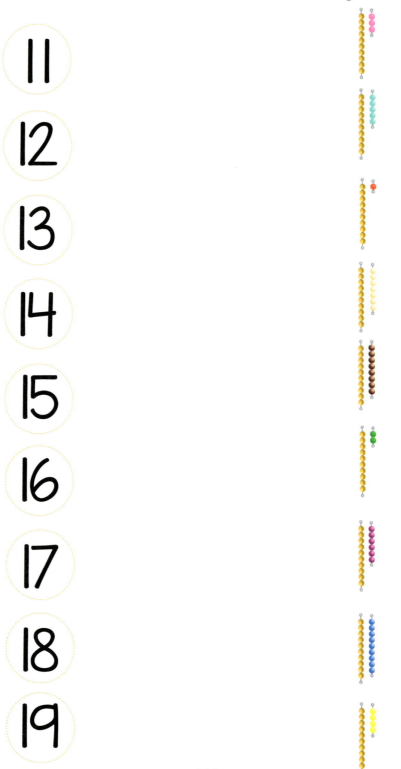

Teen Numbers - Numeral and Quantity Match

Order to mixed order. Draw a line from the beads on the left to the matching number on the right.

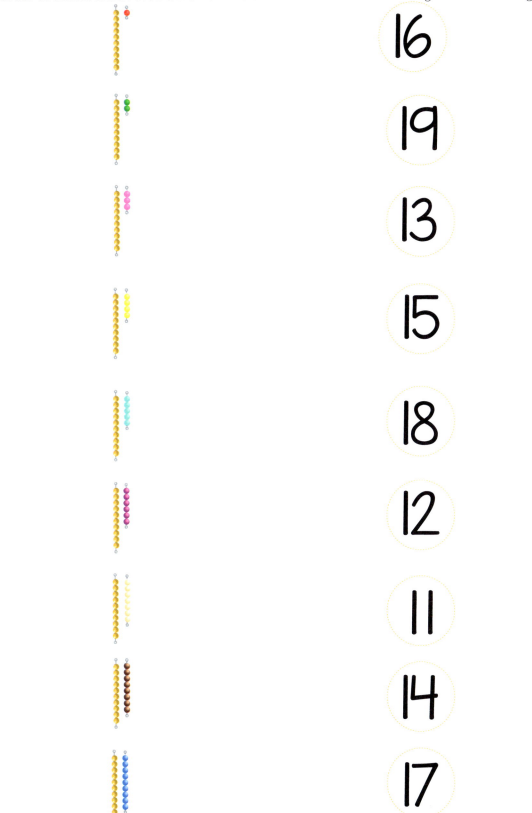

Teen Numbers - Numeral and Quantity Match

Mixed order to mixed order. Draw a line from the beads on the left to the matching number on the right.

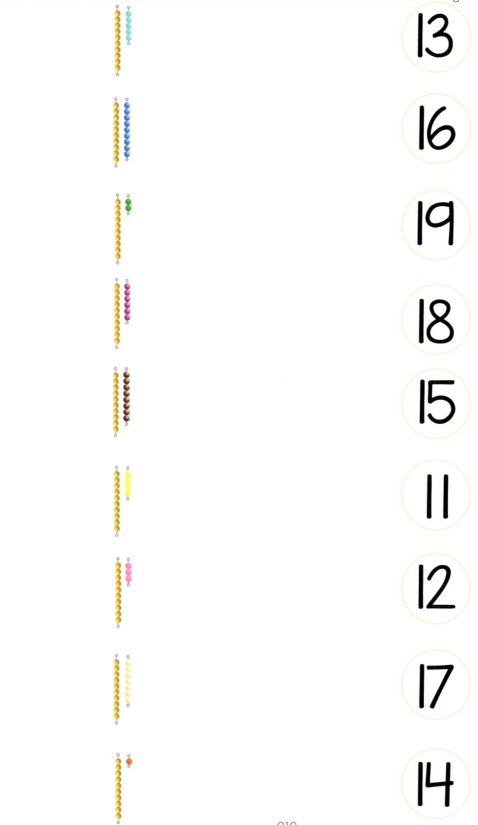

Sandpaper Teen Number Games

Game #1: Make the teen number cards "tactile" by using school glue (2:1 ratio of glue and water) and craft sand. Paint the glue onto the number, add sand, and then shake off excess. Let dry. Cut cards. Gather 19 small, identical objects to use as counters. Flip through the tactile numbers and review them in this manner:
1. First, run through the whole set of numbers once, inviting your child to trace each number with his or her pointer and middle finger while saying the name of the number.
2. Next, place a blank card on the left of workspace and number card beside it to the right. Invite your child to count out the matching number counters and place them on the blank card.
3. When the counters are next to the number, say, "There are twelve counters." Trace the number as before with your pointer and middle fingers. Say, "This says twelve."
4. Invite your child to continue in this manner for 11-19.

Game #2: Remove the tactile numbers from the workbook and place them at a far location. Ask your child to fetch each number, out of order.

Game #3: Shuffle the stack of tactile numbers. Choose a random number and ask your child to identify the numeral.

Game #4: Shuffle the stack of tactile numbers. Invite your child to place them in order 11-19.

Game #5: Give your child a random number of counters. Invite your child to retrieve matching numeral.

Game #6: Invite your child to draw the teen numbers in sand blindfolded or with his or her eyes closed. Make sure the tactile number card is traced first!

	Numbers	Date	Notes
Game 1	11 12 13 14 15 16 17 18 19		
Game 2	11 12 13 14 15 16 17 18 19		
Game 3	11 12 13 14 15 16 17 18 19		

	Numbers	Date	Notes
Game 4	11 12 13 14 15 16 17 18 19		
Game 5	11 12 13 14 15 16 17 18 19		
Game 6	11 12 13 14 15 16 17 18 19		

Key: Mark the numbers you have called and your child got correct with an "X." Mark the numbers you have called and your child did not get correct with a slash "/." Make sure to play again and call those numbers another time. When your child gets it "right" then make the full "X."

Writing Teen Numbers

First introduce the "sand tray." Give your child one tactile numeral. Your child should trace the tactile numeral three times with his or her pointer and middle fingers and then draw it in sand. Invite your child to draw as many numbers as he or she shows interest in one sitting. After all numbers have been practiced many times in sand, you can introduce the tracing sheets on the next page. Record progress on this sheet with the dates you I = Introduced the activity, A = your child Attempted the activity, and M = your child mastered the activity.

	Sand - I	Sand - A	Sand - M	Paper - I
11				
12				
13				
14				
15				
16				
17				
18				
19				

11 12

13 14

15 16

17 18

19

Writing Numbers: Tracing Sheets

219

6 6 6 6 6

7 7 7 7 7

8 8 8 8 8

9 9 9 9 9

1 2 3 4 5
6 7 8 9 10
11 12 13 14 15
16 17 18 19

Teen Number Match Game

Directions: Prep the number-bead cards by cutting off the number from the top of each card. You can use a specific cut pattern unique to each card as a control of error (variations of rounded and sharp cuts so the top will fit to the bottom like a puzzle.) There is a section for writing the number. If your child is not writing yet, you can write the number in and have your child trace your writing.

Gather: Pre-cut number-bead matching cards, a set of short bead bars to cut, the numeral cards on this page for "making the number."

Directions for "making the number:" Place a blue "10" numeral card into the box. Then place the proper numeral on top of the "0." As you demonstrate this, you should say, "Ten (place 10) and two (place 5 on top of the 0 on the 10) make fifteen." After you demonstrate, place the cards back and invite your child to do it. He or she can glue down the cards with the green digit on top in its place. There is also room to use counters, stamps, stickers, or to draw fifteen small circles.

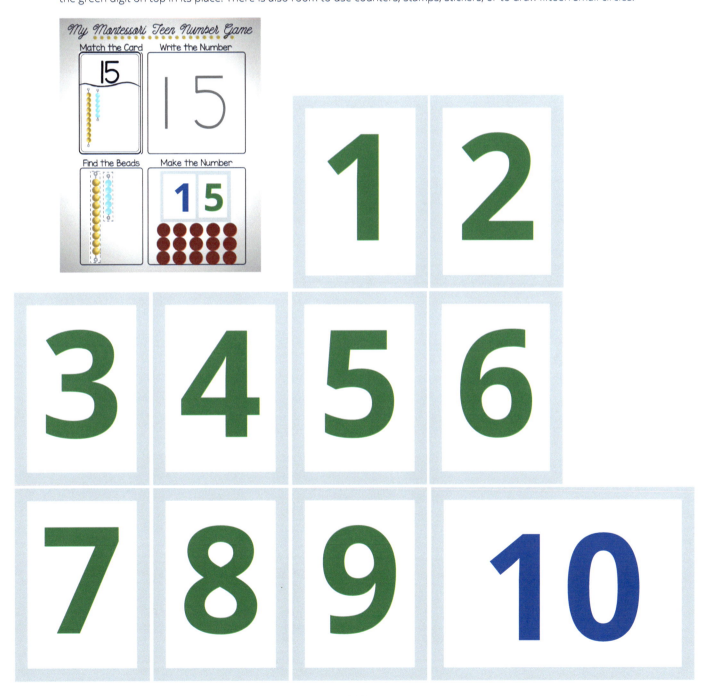

10 10

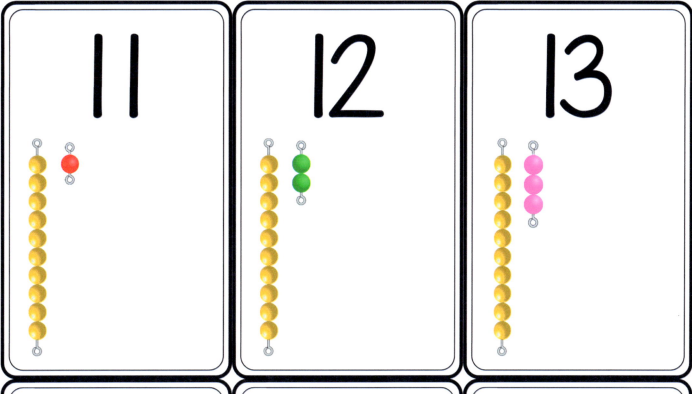

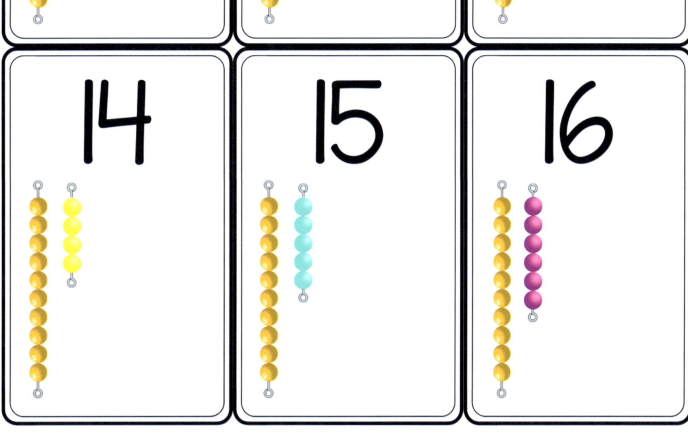

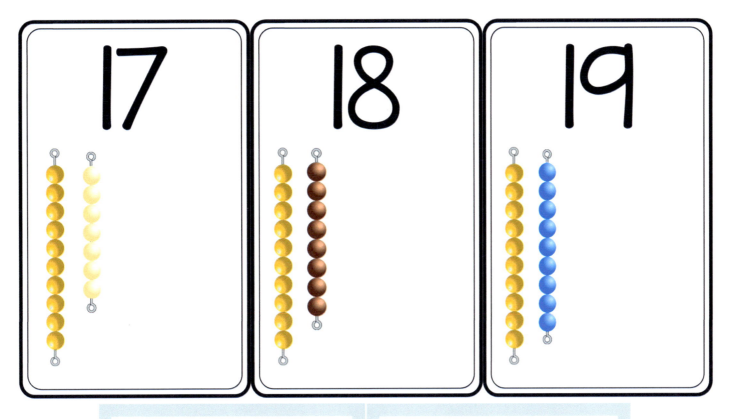
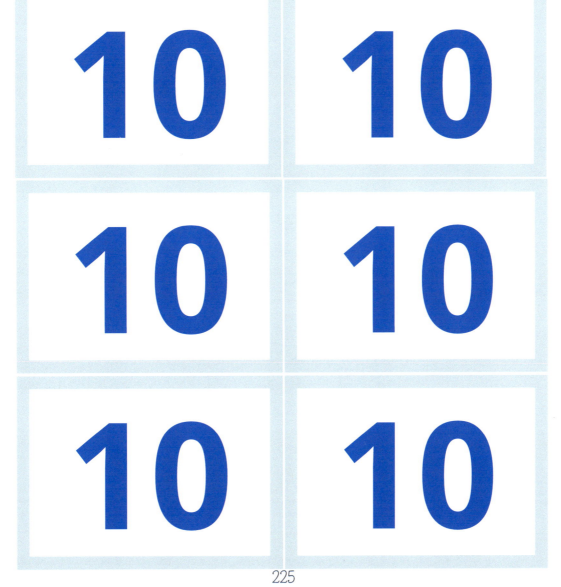

My Montessori Teen Number Game

Match the Card

Write the Number

Find the Beads

Make the Number

My Montessori Teen Number Game

Match the Card

Write the Number

Find the Beads

Make the Number

My Montessori Teen Number Game

Match the Card

Write the Number

Find the Beads

Make the Number

My Montessori Teen Number Game

Match the Card

Write the Number

Find the Beads

Make the Number

My Montessori Teen Number Game

Match the Card

Write the Number

Find the Beads

Make the Number

My Montessori Teen Number Game

Match the Card

Write the Number

Find the Beads

Make the Number

My Montessori Teen Number Game

Match the Card

Write the Number

Find the Beads

Make the Number

My Montessori Teen Number Game

Match the Card

Write the Number

Find the Beads

Make the Number

My Montessori Teen Number Game

Match the Card

Write the Number

Find the Beads

Make the Number

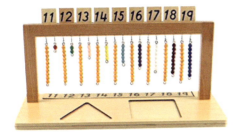

Teen Numbers

by:

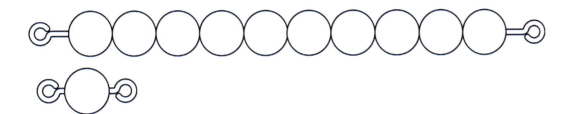

11

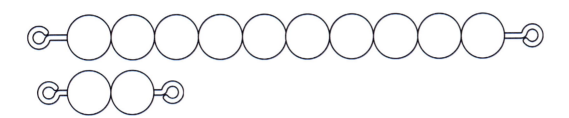

12

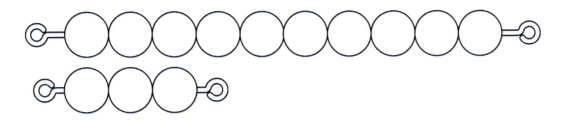

13

Directions: Print and cut along the lines. Color the bead bars the same colors as the Montessori Bead Bars. (1 = red, 2 = green, 3 = pink, 4 = yellow, 5 = light blue, 6 = purple, 7 = white, 8 = brown, 9 = dark blue, 10 = gold.) Staple together to make a booklet.

© 2020, raisingkingdomwarriors.com
Bead images by Bee Creative Clip Arts

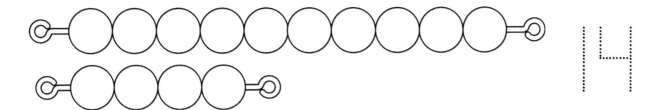 14

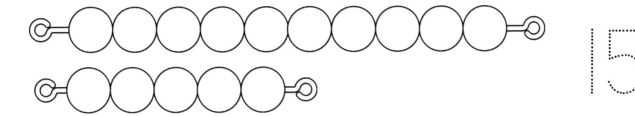 15

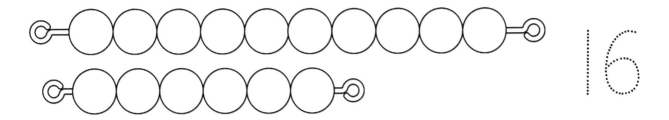 16

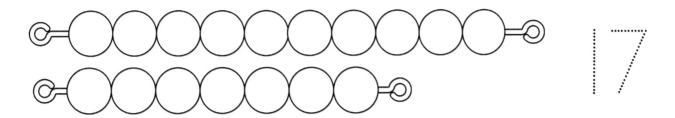 17

Directions: Print and cut along the lines. Color the bead bars the same colors as the Montessori Bead Bars. (1 = red, 2 = green, 3 = pink, 4 = yellow, 5 = light blue, 6 = purple, 7 = white, 8 = brown, 9 = dark blue, 10 = gold.) Staple together to make a booklet.

© 2020, raisingkingdomwarriors.com
Bead images by Bee Creative Clip Arts

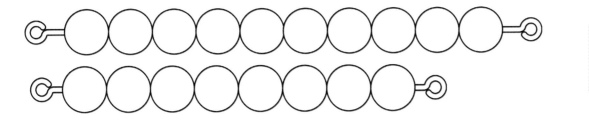

18

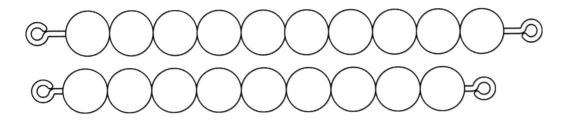

19

Directions: Print and cut along the lines. Color the bead bars the same colors as the Montessori Bead Bars. (1 = red, 2 = green, 3 = pink, 4 = yellow, 5 = light blue, 6 = purple, 7 = white, 8 = brown, 9 = dark blue, 10 = gold.) Staple together to make a booklet.

© 2020, raisingkingdomwarriors.com
Bead images by Bee Creative Clip Arts

Teens with the Number Rods

Directions: On this page, show your child how to make 11, 12, and 13 using the number rods.
1. Cut out a set of number rods for this demonstration. Align the rods on the left hand side of the work rug.
2. Bring down the Rod of 10 below the aligned set of rods. Run your finger along the Rod of Ten and say, "Ten."
3. Next, bring down the Rod of 1 and place it directly to the right of the Rod of 10, but don't let them touch yet. Say, "One."
4. Now, push them together so they are end to end. Run your finger along the Rod of 10 and say, "ten..." then along the one, "and one is eleven."
5. Repeat 3-4 for 12 and 13.
6. Invite your child to continue making 14-19, as he or she shows interest. Record which numbers have been "made" by your child.
7. Once this hands-on activity is mastered by your child, move on to the following teen number rod activities!

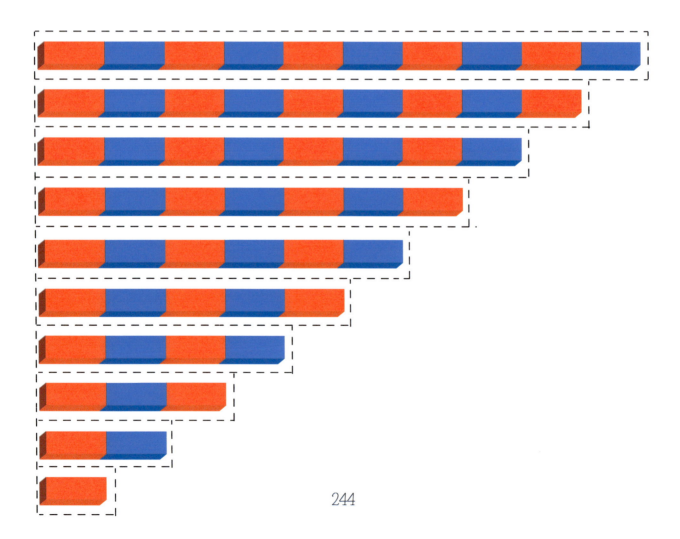

Number Rods and Cards: Make Teen Numbers

Prep the lesson by cutting (or inviting your child to cut) the set of number rods and the set of numeral cards on this page. You should have a single set of number rods 1-9, a single set of number cards 1-19, and 8 extra "10" cards. Place number rods, 1-9 cards and 11-19 cards neatly in order. Group 10 cards.

Follow this Example:

1. Show your child that the rod of 10 is in every problem. Invite your child to verify that it is the rod of ten by counting the sections.
2. Read the instructions: "Add the rod of one to the rod of ten." [Wait.] Show your child how to put it on the end.
3. What did you make? [Wait for your child to say "11."]
4. Show your child where to put the number cards. You will use "10" for every problem, then the single digit that your child added will go in the next box, and the full teen number will go in the top right corner.
5. When all is in place, verify what it says aloud by reading the number rods first. As you run your finger along the rods, say, "Ten and one equals eleven." Then verify by reading the number cards as you point to them, "Ten and one equals eleven."
6. Your child should take over and do this mostly independently. I would suggest you have your child place all the cards and/or check in with you before gluing anything down.

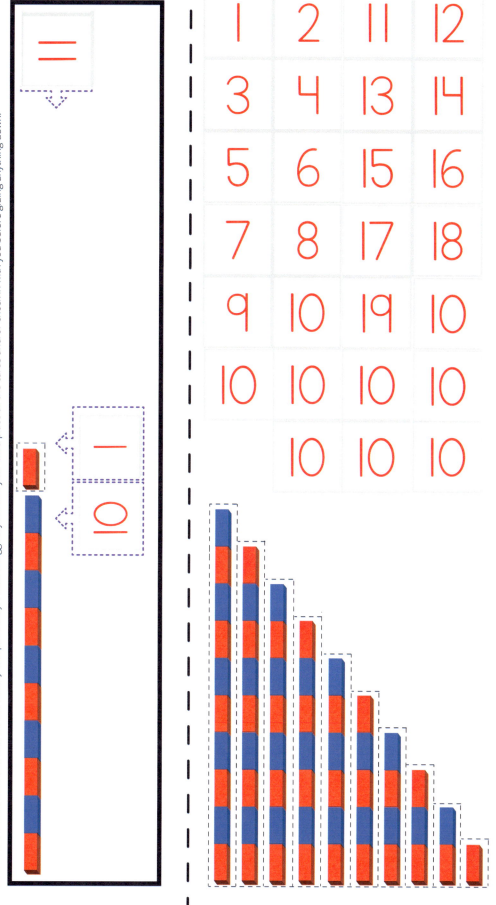

247

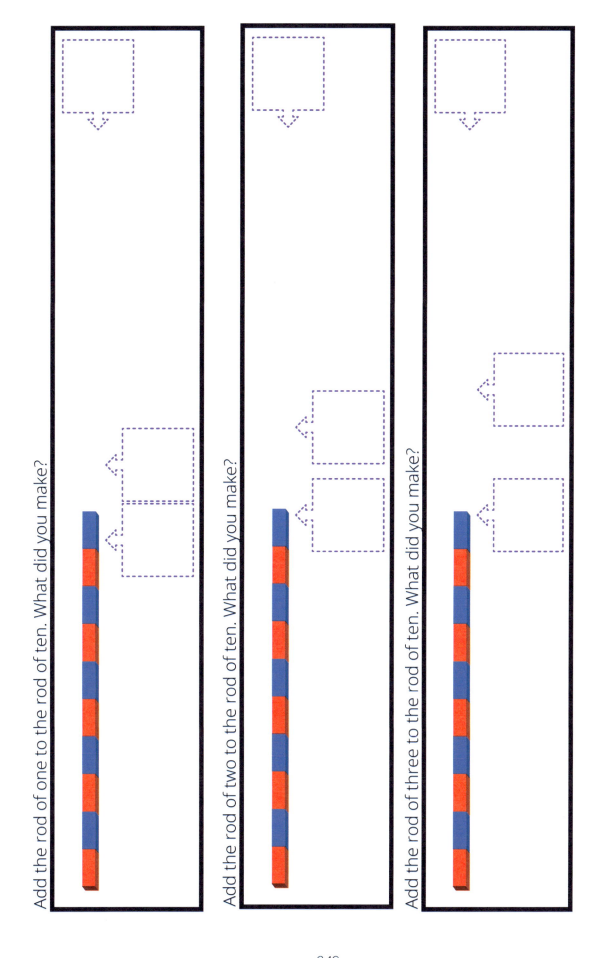

Add the rod of four to the rod of ten. What did you make?

Add the rod of five to the rod of ten. What did you make?

Add the rod of six to the rod of ten. What did you make?

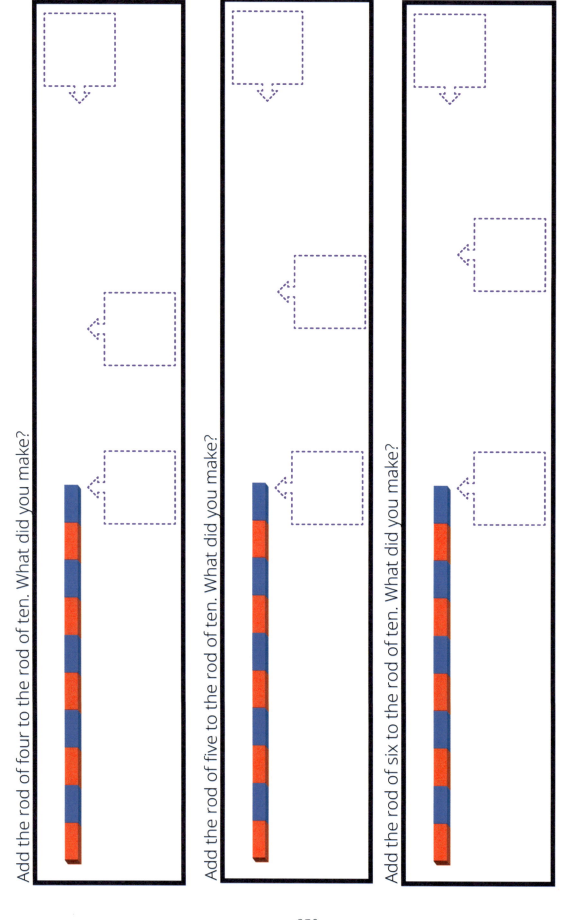

Add the rod of seven to the rod of ten. What did you make?

Add the rod of eight to the rod of ten. What did you make?

Add the rod of nine to the rod of ten. What did you make?

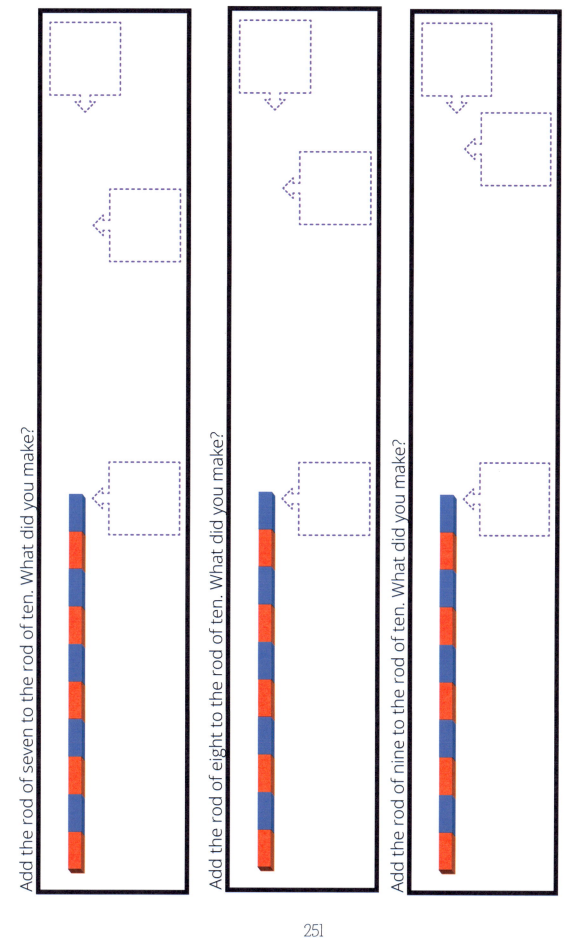

What number is this?

Directions: Circle the number that is made by joining the number rods. Then, trace the number that you circled.

1 2 3 4 5 6 7 8 9 10
11 12 13 14 15 16 17 18 19

1 2 3 4 5 6 7 8 9 10
11 12 13 14 15 16 17 18 19

1 2 3 4 5 6 7 8 9 10
11 12 13 14 15 16 17 18 19

1 2 3 4 5 6 7 8 9 10
11 12 13 14 15 16 17 18 19

1 2 3 4 5 6 7 8 9 10
11 12 13 14 15 16 17 18 19

1 2 3 4 5 6 7 8 9 10
11 12 13 14 15 16 17 18 19

1 2 3 4 5 6 7 8 9 10
11 12 13 14 15 16 17 18 19

1 2 3 4 5 6 7 8 9 10
11 12 13 14 15 16 17 18 19

1 2 3 4 5 6 7 8 9 10
11 12 13 14 15 16 17 18 19

1 2 3 4 5 6 7 8 9 10
11 12 13 14 15 16 17 18 19

1 2 3 4 5 6 7 8 9 10
11 12 13 14 15 16 17 18 19

Introduction to Tens with the Ten Boards

First Lesson: Introduce the ten numerals **by themselves**. This will be a teaching lesson, where your child should watch you carefully.
1. Open up to the Ten Boards. Point to each number in turn and say the number, "10, 20, 30, 40... 90."
2. Repeat.
3. Ask your child to say the numbers with you.
4. Say a number and ask your child to point to it. Repeat with many numbers.
5. Point to a number and ask your child to name it. Repeat with many numbers.

Note: Your child does not have to be at mastery to move on to the Second Lesson.

Second Lesson: You will need nine cut golden bead ten-bars for this lesson.
1. Open up to the Ten Boards. Lay out the nine golden bead ten-bars to the right of the workbook.
2. Point to the 10 and say, "This says ten."
3. Pick up one ten-bar and place it to the right of the 10. Say, "This is ten."
4. Point to the 20 and say, "This says twenty."
5. Pull down the ten-bar you had placed to the right of the 10 and put it to the right of the 20. Place another ten-bar next to it so they are aligned side by side, like this: ||. Say, "This is two tens, or twenty."
6. Repeat the action of pointing to the number, saying, "This says ___," pulling down the previous beads and adding another and saying, "This is ___ tens, or ____."

Child's Activity: After introducing the beads and boards in this way, invite your child to cut out a total of 45 golden bead ten bars and place the correct amount to the right of each number on the ten boards pages and glue them in place vertically, side by side.

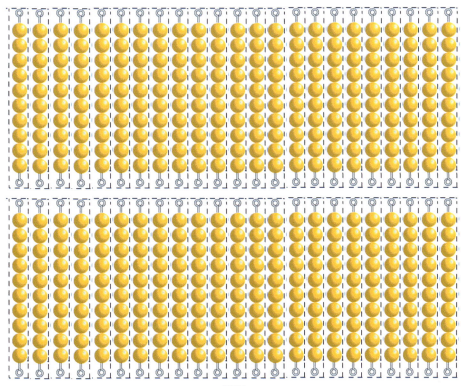

255

Ten Boards

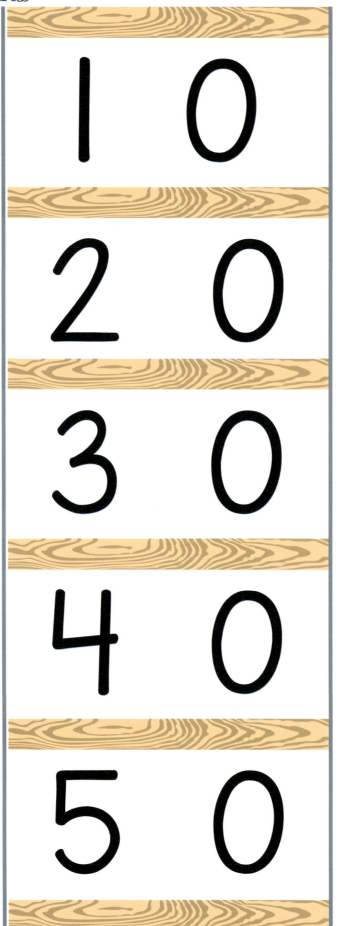

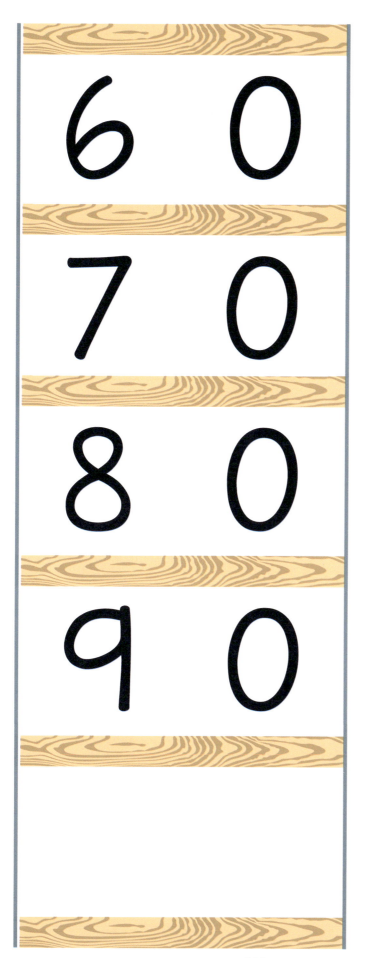

Tens - Numeral and Quantity Match

Order to mixed order. Draw a line from the number on the left to the matching beads on the right.

10

20

30

40

50

60

70

80

90

Tens - Numeral and Quantity Match

Order to mixed order. Draw a line from the number on the left to the matching beads on the right.

30

80

50

20

60

90

10

40

70

Tens - Numeral and Quantity Match

Mixed order to mixed order. Draw a line from the number on the left to the matching beads on the right.

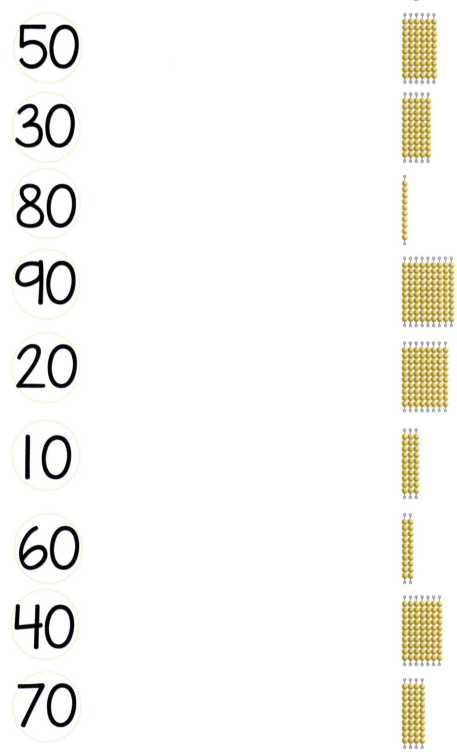

Tens: How many?

Directions: How many? Circle the number that matches the amount. Then trace the number you circled.

10 20 30 40	40 50 60 70	60 70 80 90
10 20 30 40	40 50 60 70	60 70 80 90
10 20 30 40	40 50 60 70	60 70 80 90

Finding Ten

Invite your child to draw a line from the golden bead ten-bar to the group of individual beads that make ten.

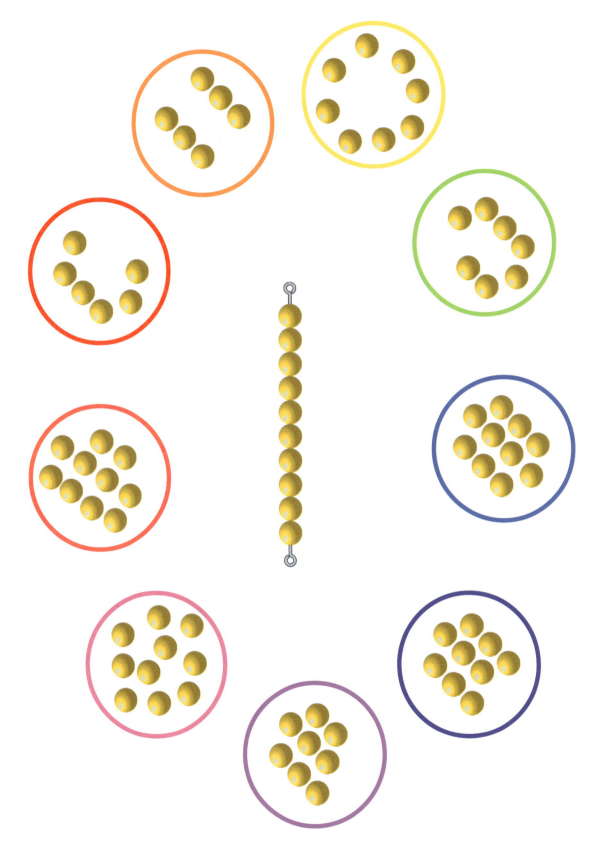

264

Counting 1-99

This lesson is a long one, but it is extremely helpful in building a foundation for later work and really understanding the *value* of each number as our children learn to count from 1 all the way to 99.

We will use the Ten Boards on the upcoming pages for this lesson, as well as the Golden Beads. You will need: 10 individual golden beads and 9 golden bead ten-bars. You will count the individual numbers 1-99 using the boards and the beads.

Directions:
1. First, cut out the 10 individual beads, 9 golden bead ten-bars, and 9 number cards with wooden strips 1-9.
2. Open up to the ten boards for this lesson.
3. Place the ten-bars to the top left of your work space, with the ten individual beads in a pile below them. Place the number cards 1-9 to the right of your workbook, aligned vertically in order with 1 on the top and 9 on the bottom.
4. Tell your child we are going to count all the way to 99 today and you need his or her help!
5. Point to the 10 on the Ten Board. Say, "This says 10." Place a ten-bar to the right. Count each bead on the ten-bar, starting at 1.
6. Ask, "What comes after 10?" [Eleven.] Add a unit bead to the right of the ten-bar. Then put the "1 card" on top of the "0" of the 10 on the Ten Board to write the number 11.
7. Grab another unit bead and place it under the previous one. Say, "twelve."
8. Replace the "1 card" with the "2 card," and point to the 12 and say, "twelve."
9. Count all the way up to 19 this way, adding a unit bead and replacing the number card. (Your child should be invited to help you!)
10. When you get to 19, add one more bead and say, "twenty." Grab a ten-bar and align it with the ten individual beads to show they are the same. Take away the ten individual beads and put them back in their original spot, essentially replacing them with the ten-bar.
11. Push the two tens into the place next to the 20 on the Ten boards. Point to the 20 and say, "twenty."
12. Keep adding unit beads, exchanging when you get ten, pushing the set of tens down to match with the next "ten" number, and continuing all the way to 99.

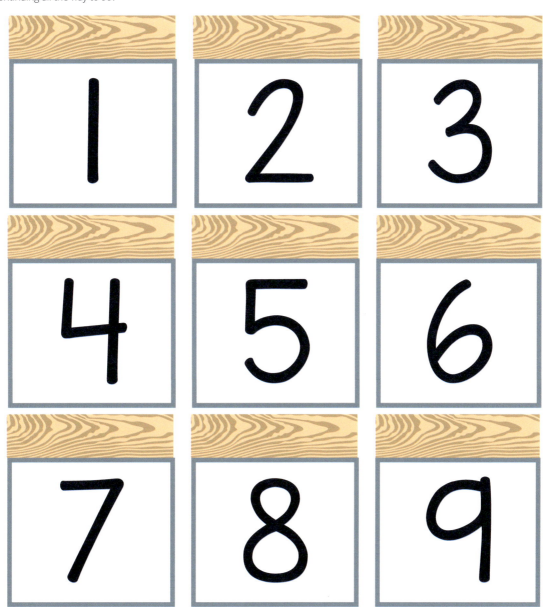

Beads for Counting 1-99
*There are TWO sets on this page for extra practice or in case any become lost.

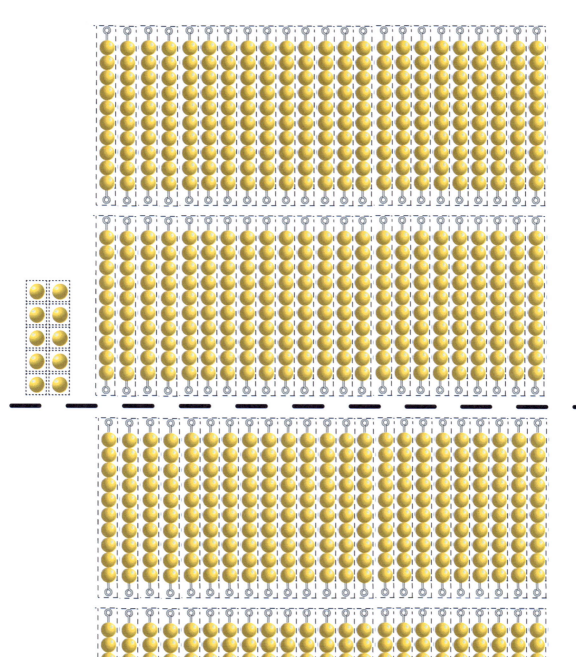

Ten Boards: Counting 1-99

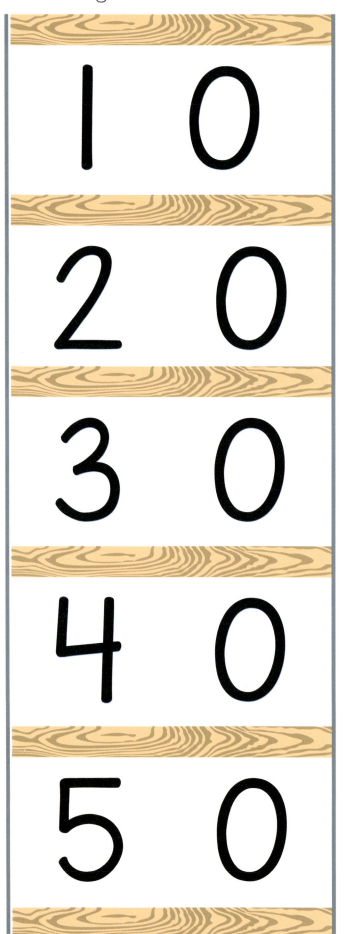

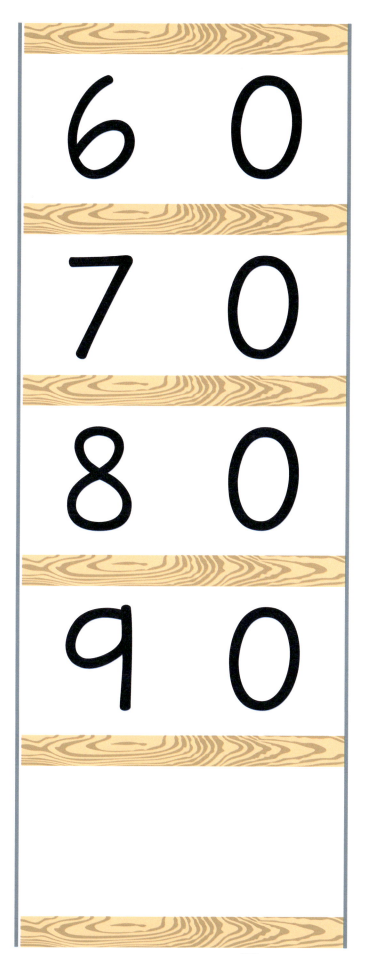

Counting 1-99 Record Keeping

It is excellent practice for your child to "make" numbers the same way you did when you taught the "Counting 1-99" lesson.
You can use this page as a record-keeping sheet to record the numbers your child has "made" using the beads and the Ten Boards.
If your child needs more direction to help him decide which numbers to make, here is an idea of how to separate this lesson:

Day 1: Make 1-10 with unit beads and number cards off to the side. Then make the exchange for "10" and move the ten-bar next to the 10 on the Ten Board. Continue through 20.
Day 2: Make 21-40.
Day 3: Make 41-70
Day 4: Make 71-99.
Day 5: Call out a random number and invite your child to count by tens to make it and then add the unit beads necessary.

NOTES: Invite your child to shade in the numbers he or she has made on this chart.

1	2	3	4	5	6	7	8	9	10
11	12	13	14	15	16	17	18	19	20
21	22	23	24	25	26	27	28	29	30
31	32	33	34	35	36	37	38	39	40
41	42	43	44	45	46	47	48	49	50
51	52	53	54	55	56	57	58	59	60
61	62	63	64	65	66	67	68	69	70
71	72	73	74	75	76	77	78	79	80
81	82	83	84	85	86	87	88	89	90
91	92	93	94	95	96	97	98	99	♥

Write the Number

Circle the number slot on the Ten Boards and the Number Card you would use to write the number value. Then write the number in the box.

Write the Number

Circle the number slot on the Ten Boards and the Number Card you would use to write the number value. Then write the number in the box.

Write the Number

Circle the number slot on the Ten Boards and the Number Card you would use to write the number value. Then write the number in the box.

Write the Number

Circle the number slot on the Ten Boards and the Number Card you would use to write the number value. Then write the number in the box.

100 Chain - Intro

Directions for Parent-:
1. First cut out the two squares of ten golden bead ten-bars and the individual arrows to have them ready. These are located on the next page.
2. Point to the full 100 square, and say, "This is one hundred."
3. Point to the 100 square with cut lines (that is right now uncut) and say, "This is one hundred."
4. Now, invite your child to carefully cut the hundred square with the cut-lines into ten golden bead ten-bars.
5. Place the intact hundred square at the top of your work space.
6. Place the individual strips of the ten-bars on top of the hundred square, showing that they match.
7. Lay out the golden bead ten-bars vertically underneath the hundred square, stretching it into a long vertical line. Tape the beads end-to-end to keep the chain intact.
8. Lay out the cut arrows in order to the right of the bead chain, stacked and ready to be placed.
9. Starting at the top bead, count individually and place the green 1-9 arrows to the right of the bead chain pointing to each bead where it belongs.
10. When you get to ten, place the blue 10 arrow. Keep counting individual beads and place the 20, 30, 40, etc. when you get to them.
11. When you get to 100, place the red 100 arrow. Then move the 100 square underneath the chain and run your finger the length of the bead chain and say, "This is one hundred." Point to the 100 square and say, "This is one hundred."

Extensions:
1. Next, count by tens from 10-100, pointing to the blue arrows as you count.
2. Count backwards by tens from 100-10, pointing to the blue arrows as you count.
3. Play "find the number!" Call out a number that is on an arrow and have your child find the number by sight or counting.

Notes:
Fold up the taped bead chain and store the 100 chain, 100 square, and individual arrows in the "pocket" you can make on this page for this exercise. You may want to place everything in a plastic sandwich bag and then into the pocket for better containment. You can take out and set up the bead chain as a control for the following 100 Chain exercises. This is also a work your child may want to do himself and return to at a later date. In Book 2, when we look at the 1000 chain, we will review this work again.

fold on this line.

fold the bottom of this page up to make a pocket to store the beads and arrows

100 Chain Exercises

Printables: Cut out the bottom part of this page for the "100 Chain - Intro" lesson. Cut out the right portion of this page for the "100 Chain Exercises" that are on the following pages.

Directions: On the next 2 pages are exercises to help your child practice the 100 Chain.

"My 100 Chain" Instructions for Your Child:
1. Invite your child to cut one set of blue arrows 10-90 and one 100 arrow.
2. Your child should arrange the arrows in order to the right of the workbook, vertically with "10" on the top and "100" on the bottom.
3. Invite your child to first draw an arrow from each green arrow on the page to the bead to which the number corresponds.
4. Tell your child to place the blue arrows and red arrow in their proper spots along the chain.
5. After verifying the accuracy of the placement of the arrows with the control (100 chain you set out previously), your child can glue the arrows in place.

100 Chain Cut and Paste:
Your child should cut out one set of green arrows, one set of blue arrows, and four red 100 arrows. Arrange them. Then paste them into their appropriate spots on each of the four 100 chains. There will be leftover green arrows.

This section is for "100 Chain Intro"

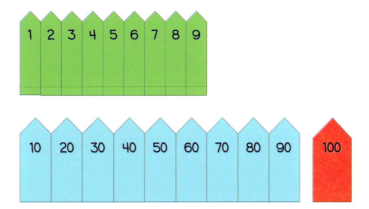

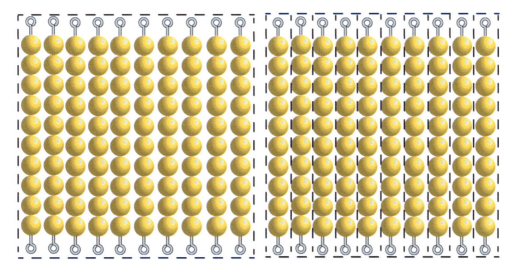

Draw a line from each green arrow to its matching bead.

Place the following arrows on this side of the bead chain then glue them in place: 10, 20, 30, 40, 50, 60, 70, 80, 90, 100.

My 100 Chain

100 Chain Cut and Paste

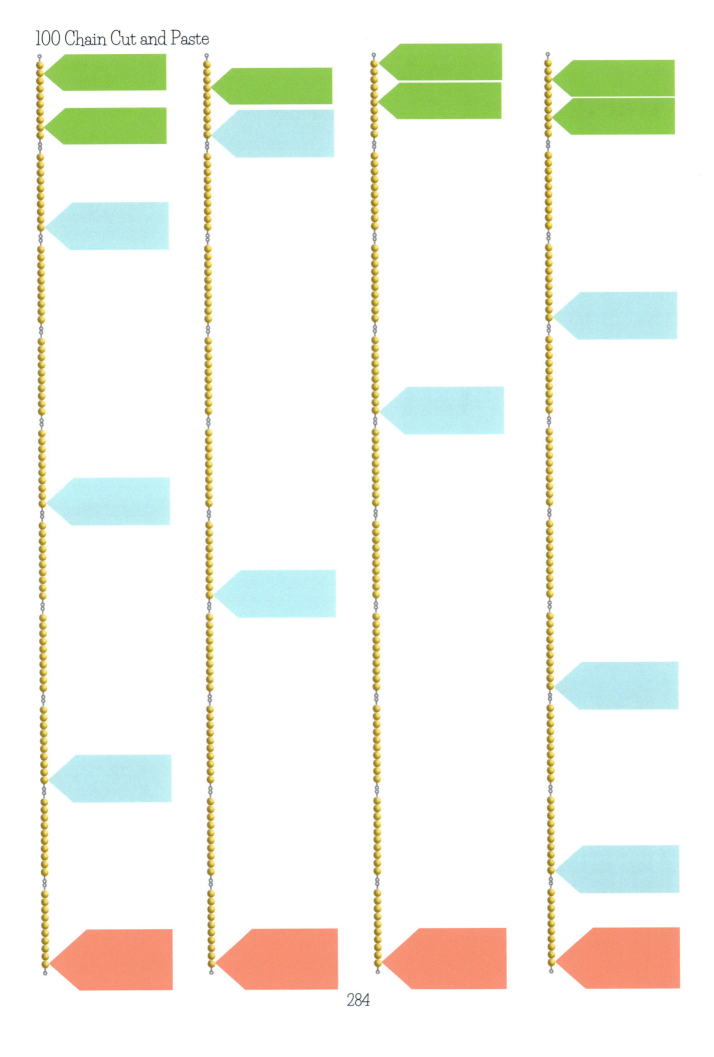

Hundred Board - Intro

This is another large lesson, and it may take several sittings to get the hundred board completed. I have included extra Hundred Board cut and paste lessons for children who want or need more work with this lesson. Print as many Hundred Boards and Number cards as needed! (This page and the next one.)

Directions:
1. Cut the number cards on this page in strips 1-10, 11-20, etc. Only use one strip at a time.
2. Cut apart the number strip you want to work on today into individual number cards.
3. Mix them up, then invite your child to arrange them, in order, along the proper horizontal row.
4. Check the "Hundred Board Control Chart" as needed.
5. After verifying with the Control Chart, glue the individual number cards in place.
6. Continue until entire board is filled.

Extension 1: Mix up 20 number cards at a time.
Extension 2: Pick a random number tile from all 1-100 tiles and have your child place it where it belongs on the chart.

1	2	3	4	5	6	7	8	9	10
11	12	13	14	15	16	17	18	19	20
21	22	23	24	25	26	27	28	29	30
31	32	33	34	35	36	37	38	39	40
41	42	43	44	45	46	47	48	49	50
51	52	53	54	55	56	57	58	59	60
61	62	63	64	65	66	67	68	69	70
71	72	73	74	75	76	77	78	79	80
81	82	83	84	85	86	87	88	89	90
91	92	93	94	95	96	97	98	99	100

Hundred Board Control Chart

1	2	3	4	5	6	7	8	9	10
11	12	13	14	15	16	17	18	19	20
21	22	23	24	25	26	27	28	29	30
31	32	33	34	35	36	37	38	39	40
41	42	43	44	45	46	47	48	49	50
51	52	53	54	55	56	57	58	59	60
61	62	63	64	65	66	67	68	69	70
71	72	73	74	75	76	77	78	79	80
81	82	83	84	85	86	87	88	89	90
91	92	93	94	95	96	97	98	99	100

raisingkingdomwarriors.com

Trace the Numbers 1-100

1	2	3	4	5	6	7	8	9	10
11	12	13	14	15	16	17	18	19	20
21	22	23	24	25	26	27	28	29	30
31	32	33	34	35	36	37	38	39	40
41	42	43	44	45	46	47	48	49	50
51	52	53	54	55	56	57	58	59	60
61	62	63	64	65	66	67	68	69	70
71	72	73	74	75	76	77	78	79	80
81	82	83	84	85	86	87	88	89	90
91	92	93	94	95	96	97	98	99	100

Trace the Numbers 1-100

1	2	3	4	5	6	7	8	9	10
11	12	13	14	15	16	17	18	19	20
21	22	23	24	25	26	27	28	29	30
31	32	33	34	35	36	37	38	39	40
41	42	43	44	45	46	47	48	49	50
51	52	53	54	55	56	57	58	59	60
61	62	63	64	65	66	67	68	69	70
71	72	73	74	75	76	77	78	79	80
81	82	83	84	85	86	87	88	89	90
91	92	93	94	95	96	97	98	99	100

Hundred Board Fill-in-the-Blank

There are three hundred boards with "missing" number tiles. Either cut and paste this hundred chart to use the numbers to fill in the tiles or write in the missing tiles. Use the Hundred Board Control Chart to check your work!

1	2	3	4	5	6	7	8	9	10
11	12	13	14	15	16	17	18	19	20
21	22	23	24	25	26	27	28	29	30
31	32	33	34	35	36	37	38	39	40
41	42	43	44	45	46	47	48	49	50
51	52	53	54	55	56	57	58	59	60
61	62	63	64	65	66	67	68	69	70
71	72	73	74	75	76	77	78	79	80
81	82	83	84	85	86	87	88	89	90
91	92	93	94	95	96	97	98	99	100

Write or paste in the missing numbers.

1	2	3	4		6	7	8	9	10
11		13	14	15	16	17	18	19	20
21	22	23	24	25		27	28	29	30
	32	33	34	35	36	37	38	39	40
41	42	43	44	45	46	47	48	49	
51	52	53	54	55	56	57		59	60
61	62		64	65	66	67	68	69	70
71	72	73	74	75	76	77	78		80
81	82	83		85	86	87	88	89	90
91	92	93	94	95	96		98	99	100

Write or paste in the missing numbers.

1	2	3	4	5		7	8	9	10
11	12		14	15	16	17	18	19	20
21	22	23	24	25	26	27		29	30
31		33	34	35	36	37	38	39	40
41	42	43	44	45	46		48	49	50
51	52	53	54		56	57	58	59	60
61	62	63		65	66	67	68	69	70
71	72	73	74	75	76	77	78	79	
	82	83	84	85	86	87	88	89	90
91	92	93	94	95	96	97	98		100

Write or paste in the missing numbers.

1	2	3	4	5	6	7	8	9	
11	12	13	14		16	17	18	19	20
21	22	23	24	25	26	27	28		30
31	32		34	35	36		38	39	40
	42	43	44	45	46	47	48	49	50
51	52	53		55	56	57	58	59	60
61		63	64	65	66	67	68	69	70
71	72	73	74	75	76	77		79	80
81	82	83	84	85	86	87	88	89	90
91	92	93	94	95		97	98	99	100

Write or paste in the missing numbers.

1	2		4	5	6	7	8	9	10
11	12	13	14	15		17	18	19	20
21	22	23	24		26	27	28	29	30
31	32	33	34	35	36	37	38		40
41	42	43	44	45	46	47		49	50
	52	53	54	55	56	57	58	59	60
61	62	63	64	65	66		68	69	70
71	72	73		75	76	77	78	79	80
81	82	83	84	85	86	87	88	89	90
91		93	94	95	96	97	98	99	

Write the Numbers 1-100

Write the Numbers 1-100

Name:_____

Date Completed:_____

Book 1 Completed

I can count 0-100!

Dear _____,

You did it! You worked hard and completed your **Montessori Math Workbook, Book 1!** I am most proud of you for _____.

I love how you _____
_____.

You have proven you are capable of
_____!

Most of all, I want you to know that I love you, and we are on this journey together, every step of the way.

Love, _____

Made in the USA
Columbia, SC
05 March 2025